JOHN WALDEN

MEMOIRS
of a Moonraker

A LIFE IN AND OUT OF BUSINESS

JOHN WALDEN

MEMOIRS
of a Moonraker

A LIFE IN AND OUT OF BUSINESS

MEMOIRS

CIRENCESTER

Mereo Books

1A The Wool Market Dyer Street Cirencester Gloucestershire GL7 2PR
An imprint of Memoirs Publishing www.mereobooks.com

Memoirs of a Moonraker: 978-1-86151-340-3

First published in Great Britain in 2014
by Mereo Books, an imprint of Memoirs Publishing

The address for Memoirs Publishing Group Limited can be found at
www.memoirspublishing.com

The Memoirs Publishing Group Ltd Reg. No. 7834348

Cover design - Ray Lipscombe

The Memoirs Publishing Group supports both The Forest Stewardship Council® (FSC®) and
the PEFC® leading international forest-certification organisations. Our books carrying both the
FSC label and the PEFC® and are printed on FSC®-certified paper. FSC® is the only
forest-certification scheme supported by the leading environmental organisations including
Greenpeace. Our paper procurement policy can be found at
www.memoirspublishing.com/environment

Typeset in 11/15pt Bembo
by Wiltshire Associates Publisher Services Ltd. Printed and bound in Great Britain by
Printondemand-Worldwide, Peterborough PE2 6XD

PREFACE

These memoirs cover the life of John Walden (JW) and include a history of the Walden family business from the time when the founder, the author's father, Henry Walden, arrived in Trowbridge, Wiltshire, in 1926. 'Moonraker' is a colloquial name for a Wiltshire person, derived from an 18th century tale about a group of smugglers who were trying to retrieve barrels of hidden contraband from the bottom of the village pond when they were surprised by the excise men. They fooled the men by pretending that they thought the moon's reflection was a cheese and were trying to rake it in to the bank.

CONTENTS

Foreword

Introduction

Acknowledgements

FOREWORD

by the Marquis of Lansdowne

One of my regrets as I approach three score years and thirteen is failing to keep a diary. Memories can be short. With the effluxion of time, one decade merges into the next. We know that an event happened around a certain time, but the precise details become blurred. Once lost, they are usually lost forever.

John's autobiography reminds us of the days before the advent of supermarkets when small retail operations flourished, the pace of life moved rhythmically and Sundays were special. The day before the pace of life was transformed by universal mobility and the development of the internet.

This short preface may suggest that John has not moved with the times. How wrong this would be. Not only is his retentive memory remarkable, but he is also still young at heart. Something to be envied.

All ages will enjoy reading these memoirs. For some it will be a reminder of earlier times; for the majority a fascinating glimpse of the past.

Bowood House, the home of the Marquis and Marchioness of Lansdowne

INTRODUCTION

In 2008, while recuperating after a three-year period of ill health, I prepared some draft material for a book covering my life. Some years later, on a visit to my birthplace, Trowbridge in Wiltshire, I was quite disappointed to see that the last trace of the Walden family and their Walden business, which spanned some 70 years, was being removed. This was the name 'WALDENS' displayed in bold block letters on the end of a large cold store at Ladydown at the bottom of Canal Road. This was one of several cold stores which I had built some twenty or more years previously. The new owners, apetito, were painting over the name as I looked on. Luckily I had my camera with me and took a photo – see chapter 10.

This has given me two reasons to make the effort - first to try and prepare a "jolly good read" for my many friends and relations, and secondly to encourage the Trowbridge powers that be to give Waldens some recognition, not only of its existence but of the prosperity the Walden family brought to the town and beyond, both in my time and subsequently.

I have, by and large, had a fantastic life and I am very grateful, at the ripe age of 82, that I am in good shape for the task. I have never kept a diary, but fortunately my memory is extraordinary.

My main theme is my 35 years as a Director, firstly of Waldens of Trowbridge Ltd from 1952–1962 and then as Managing Director of Waldens Wiltshire Foods Ltd, 1963 –2006. This was followed by the establishment of an international campsite, Blackland Lakes, at Calne, also in Wiltshire.

But my book is by no means all about the 'daily grind'. My stories are of the many people I have met, both in business and privately, plus many of the highlights of an interesting and eventful life, particularly my experiences in Canada and the USA and the great pleasure I have enjoyed with riding and sailing. I hope you enjoy reading it as much as I have enjoyed writing it. I am not normally known for blowing my own trumpet, and I apologise if I have blown it too hard in one or two instances!

John Walden | January 2015

ACKNOWLEDGEMENTS

I am very pleased to acknowledge the help and encouragement I received from my late brother Michael, his wife Gillian and my special daughter Sarah who lives across the Pond, in Florida USA. Michael, right up to the time he "departed", had a great long-term memory and filled in many gaps where my memory was lacking.

Additionally, I would like to record the help given by my younger brother Ben, who kindly dug out some early photos of the Walden business. Also, Dennis Gerrish, who assisted with my chapter on the Walden, refrigerated transport business, Frigfreight Ltd.

My Editor, Chris Newton, the Editor-in-Chief of Memoir Publishing, has been a tower of strength. He needed a lot of patience, particularly as this has been my first effort!

My IT expert, Mike Sanderson, of Forest Edge Computer services, has been a terrific help. I am now able to "control" my IT machinery far better than when I began writing in 2012. I am indebted to Lord Lansdowne, who very kindly provided the foreword (See Chapter 12). I must thank my great friend Martin Pound RN Rtd., who suggested that I should write my memoirs in the first place. Also, John and Wendy Richardson, who read my chapter on sailing. I recall that John said it was a "good read", which encouraged me to keep writing!

I have thoroughly enjoyed my writing and I sincerely hope that you will enjoy reading the result of my efforts.

I wish you all good health, peace, prosperity and a happy future.

John Walden | February 2015

CHAPTER 1

THE FOUNDING OF A COMPANY - WALDENS OF TROWBRIDGE, 1926-1952

Waldens arrived in Trowbridge in 1926 when the founder, Henry John Walden, set up business on the outskirts of Trowbridge. 'Great oaks from little acorns grow', and Waldens began as a very little acorn. Prior to 1926 Henry had been apprenticed to an uncle in East Coker, Somerset, who owned a butter factory. In 1926 he set up his own quite small factory to make butter behind the Lion and Fiddle public house in Hilperton, near Trowbridge.

Soon his father Herbert joined him. Herbert was a natural salesman and I remember him in his bowler hat and smoking his pipe. Henry bought the milk from the farmers, separated the cream, and made it into butter. Herbert sold it to local shops. Shortly Henry was joined by his younger brother, Leslie, who added to the sales force. I am told by Leslie's daughter, Gillian, that her father delivered the butter to local shops on a motorbike and sidecar. I understand that a photo exists showing two

1

young men, Henry and Leslie, 'leaning over a motor bike and sidecar, chatting away, nonchalantly'. Probably not such a good machine as the one below!

A 1926 Norton Model 18 500cc sidecar outfit. I very much doubt if Leslie had one as good as this!

The business prospered and a limited company was established, Waldens Mid Wilts Creameries Ltd. Around 1928 Henry had a purpose-built factory constructed on The Down, Trowbridge. Shortly after, next to the butter factory, he had a house (Downside, 62 The Down), built for himself and his new wife Phyllis Harriet (née Brunt) who he married in about May 1931. I was their first son, born in January 1932. Michael followed a year later and Ben six years later.

Apparently a Gus Hawker sold Henry a business which was probably based in this building at the rear of the Lion and Fiddle. Gus had immigrated to Canada, married a Red Indian squaw and become very rich, as he found uranium!

Herbert John Walden

Henry John Walden

Henry's younger brother, Leslie Gordon. Photo
extracted from the firm's outing to Weymouth, 1936

This is the building, behind the Lion and Fiddle Pub at Hilperton, where Henry Walden made butter and
founded Waldens of Trowbridge in 1926. Photo by JW, 2014

A photo of the Walden factory next to Downside, The Down (1936). JW in the racing car and Michael on his mother Phyllis Walden's knee. No larger photo of the factory can be found.

Part of the front of the Walden factory, showing the offices to the right (1950). The first garage is on the left - it later became the egg packing station before it was moved to Ladydown. JW's first proper car, an MG TD, in front.

Originally the butter was sold in round half-pound packs which were rolled by hand. Mechanisation came later in the new factory on the Down.

I do recall that a Mr Harold Lemon, a solicitor from the Swindon firm of Lemon, Humphrey and Parker, regularly attended meetings with Henry. I am sure he was able to help with the early financing of the business. I believe that the National Westminster Bank was also a great help.

5

All manufacturing businesses should establish a brand name for their products. My father was aware of this and was considering what name he should give the half-pound retail packs of butter. One day Jim Brunt, a pig farmer at Hullavington, who was married to one of Henry's sisters, Floss, visited the factory. Henry, straight out of the blue, decided that 'Farmer Jim' would be just right as a name for the butter. This proved to be a brilliant move and was used initially for butter, and later for poultry. A photo of Herbert was used on the packaging, both of butter and at a later date, poultry, mainly chicken.

The first share certificate. Note the directors are Henry Walden and Harold Lemon. The Secretary is Geoffrey Norris, who, apart from wartime service in the RAF, was a very valuable member of Staff until his retirement in about 1983.

Over the years prior to World War 2 various other departments were added and additional buildings were erected on the two-acre site. One housed a butchery which turned out excellent sausages. Herbert Hayward was the chief butcher and was on parade at six each morning. As we were living close by we were awakened by his whistling each morning, rather like a cock crowing. Occasionally his enthusiasm got the better of him and the sausages either had too much, or too little, salt or pepper!

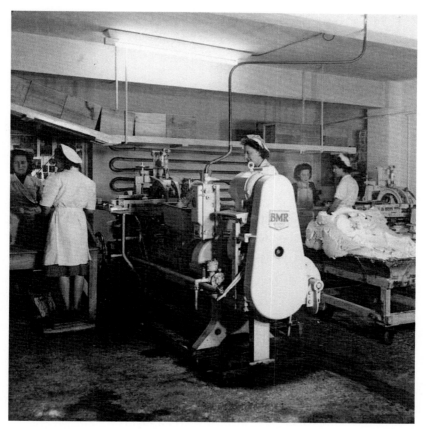

The butter packing machines in the new factory on The Down. The butter arrived, very solid, mostly from New Zealand. It was blended in an adjoining area to make it fit to pass through the packing machines.

Waldens' Butchery Department. Herbert Hayward is 2nd from right next to Denis Pearce. Circa 1937

Apparently Herbert was addicted to gambling, and a few years later he must have got into serious trouble with the bookies. He had 'lost his shirt' and much more besides. He failed to turn up for work and a couple of weeks later his body was found in Biss Woods towards West Ashton, where he had died from hypothermia (or hanged from a tree?) I have avoided gambling ever since I heard this!

As time went on there were several members of different families working at Waldens. One was the Pearce family; 'Pop' Pearce, who stoked the large boiler to raise steam and kept the site tidy, and his three sons, Howard, who with a special cutting wire, cut the cheese and packed it to order and the other two were butchers, Dennis and Tony.

By 1939 the variety of products was quite extensive and included various freshly-baked pies, pasties, and sausage rolls. Initially all the meat required for the pie fillings would have been prepared in the Butchery Department. I recall that the Ministry of Food had set standards for the meat content of pies, and all food was regularly checked to see if the correct standards were adhered to. Waldens generally kept to the rules. However on one occasion in the late 50s we received a summons to appear before Trowbridge Magistrates because we failed to include the correct amount of kidney in our steak and kidney pies. This was a silly mistake, as it would be much cheaper for the firm to include the correct amount of kidney, which is far cheaper than steak. I represented the company and stood in the dock. We were fined a modest sum and we made sure that the problem was corrected immediately.

A wide range of cakes eventually became a major product and a very skilled confectionery baker was engaged, a Mr White, who together with his son, Tony, proved to be a great asset. All sections prospered. A fleet of vans was gradually purchased, manned by van salesmen. The sales area was extended, and, in addition to the vans which were based at Trowbridge, others were added at Andover, Woking, Swindon and Bournemouth. Among the van salesmen were Arthur Seymour (who was married to another of Henry's sisters, my Aunt Margery), Paul Stumbles, Ray Ward, Bill Wheeler, Frank Cordey, Dickie Wilson, Harry Fielding, Archie Collis and Robert Wyatt.

When the new factory on the Down was built, rather than make the butter it was bought in bulk (56lb cartons). A large proportion came from New Zealand. It needed to be blended and packed in half-pound packets. All this was done with modern machines and packed in 'Farmer Jim' brand wrappers supplied by F Slugg and Co, printers in Trowbridge. I think about 20 tons were packed per week. George T. Brown, hauliers, of Steeple Ashton, regularly delivered the bulk cartons of butter to the factory, having collected them from Avonmouth Docks. Prior to this it would have been delivered from Trowbridge Railway Station by Great Western Railway using three-wheel tractors and trailers. Even earlier, I remember, GWR were making deliveries with a horse and cart.

Initially, a large garage had been erected next to the main factory to accommodate and maintain the expanding fleet of vans. Soon this had to be vacated as Henry had purchased an egg packing business from a Mr Williams of Bath, who remained Manager until his retirement. Shortly after this development, WW2 broke out and as a wartime measure the collection of eggs was zoned so that eggs from all producers (both large and small) within a 15-mile or so radius were collected by Waldens.

Mr Williams's retirement ceremony. From the left: Gordon Read, Henry Walden, John Walden, Michael Walden, Mr Williams and Ben Walden. Circa 1958

As a young lad, around 10 to 12 years old, I used to accompany the egg collection drivers in the school holidays. I got to know the area and many of the farmers quite well. One driver I was particularly fond of was Albert 'Col' Blake, a retired farmer. On each of his daily rounds, he had a favourite pub where he would stop for a pint, eat his sandwiches and have a nap!

I recall that there was one egg collection driver called Mr Phyllis, who was an active communist. He approached me one day and told me that when the next socialist government was elected and Waldens was nationalized, I would be employed. Fortunately for me, and everyone else working for Waldens and for the country at large, this did not materialize, but it was touch and go, and had it happened it would have been a major disaster.

Around this time my father gave me his views on politics. Although he generally supported the Conservatives, as I have and still do, he stressed that it was always necessary to have a good opposition to ensure that extreme and harmful policies were avoided. I fully agree with this. It was, and is, essential to prevent the country from lurching too far to the right or left. Henry was on Trowbridge Council for many years and he sat as an Independent!

One advantage of having the egg packing station next to where we lived was that there were always hundreds of wooden egg collection boxes stacked in the factory yard. Michael and I used them to build private dens in which to play and hide! Also the road around the factory was just right for travelling at speed on a four-wheel cart which Father made for us. These activities were, of course, only practised when the factory was closed, when Michael and I were about five or six years old.

When I was about 16 I sometimes helped the Wages Clerk, a Miss Adlam, who was quite a formidable character but good at her job. All the wages were paid each Friday in cash and the Company Secretary, Geoffrey Norris, would tour the various departments and hand out the wage packets. It was very rare for anyone to be handed an incorrect amount.

I remember a few of the other office staff; one was Betty Long, who operated a comptometer, the forerunner of the computer. Betty was very quick and accurate with this machine, with which she daily checked all the van sales men's Invoices. Joyce Barrett was the receptionist and telephone operator. Several attractive and pleasant Polish girls from one family were employed, together with their father, a Mr

Swiderski, who had lost both legs in WW2. The switchboard was a massive unit with dozens of cords which had to be plugged in to the extensions. Many years later the first computer was purchased. This nearly took up a whole room and measured about four feet by two! The computer operator was Brenda Walden, wife of my cousin Donald, who later became the firm's accountant.

Henry was quite an astute businessman and was honest, diligent and progressive. He treated his staff well and was well liked. It was widely known that if a new employee survived the first two weeks working for Henry, he or she, could well be there for the rest of their working lives.

Every year Henry organised a staff outing to the seaside, and in the early days one or more open charabancs were hired. The favourite destinations were Swanage and Weymouth. After WW2 had ended a whole train was hired, and I went on two outings by rail, one to Southsea and the other to Paignton. All were very popular and kept morale high; Waldens was a happy ship.

At about this time the company's name was changed to Waldens of Trowbridge Ltd to take account of the fact that a much wider range of products were now dealt with.

The firm's outing to Weymouth or Swanage, 1936. Those who I can recognise: Far left, Harry Fielding. Back row: 3rd along, Howard Pearce, 9th Ray Ward, Gordon Read, Arthur Seymour. 'Pop' Pearce in bowler hat. Far right: Eileen and Ron Courtier. Middle front row: Bill Walden with Archie Collis just behind him. End of front row: Leslie Walden.

Another outing: 1936. Again, those I can recognise: 2nd row from the back row, 5th along Ray Ward, Howard Pearce, Archie Collis, Bill Walden and his wife, Frank Alford, and at the end of the row, Ron Courtier. Front row: From left, Dorothy and Geoffrey Norris, Herbert Hayward, possibly Margery Seymour, Phyllis and Henry John Walden, Herbert John Walden with Pipe. Behind and between Henry and Herbert John are Doreen and George Shipway. (Doreen worked in the butchery dept. and George Shipway helped Arthur Seymour at Andover.)

In 1939 when WW2 started, Henry, now nearly forty, was given reserved occupation status, which made him exempt from military service. His job was to help keep the nation fed, which was vital for the war effort. More and more troops moved into Wiltshire, especially on and around Salisbury Plain, which was, and still is, the main military training area in the UK. This was primarily in readiness for the D-Day Landings in Normandy, France.

One of the main activities of Waldens at this time was the production of steak and kidney pies, which were turned out by the thousand. Often an Army lorry would arrive to collect a load. The NAAFI were major customers. Waldens' pies would have been shipped around the world to feed troops and sailors at sea. Troops were billeted in many houses in Trowbridge, including Downside, The Down. Henry moved his family to a smaller house in The Croft. In 1942/3 thousands of American troops arrived. I don't think their diet included Waldens steak and kidney pies!

Aunt Maud, one of Henry's sisters (the prettiest!) was very popular with American officers. I met several of them and they were especially friendly and generous to me. One, a captain, together with a friend of mine, took us for a ride in his tank on Salisbury Plain, near Tilshead, where they were encamped and training for D-Day. This especially nice man was one of the many thousands who lost their lives in Normandy.

Waldens' Egg Packing Station after it was moved to Ladydown from The Down in about 1960. At this time it was managed by Michael Walden.

A group photo taken in Trowbridge Civic Hall about 1960. Back row on left: Mr Williams, Henry Walden, Ann Walden, John Walden. Seated on left: Phyllis Walden, Ben Walden, Jennifer Walden, next two unknown, Gordon and Joan Read. Bottom two unknown. Seated right: Gillian Walden, Michael Walden, Dorothy Norris, Geoffrey Norris, and Paul Stumbles. Rest unknown.

CHAPTER 2

MY EARLY LIFE, 1932-1952

I was born at Downside, 62 The Down, Trowbridge, and delivered by a very experienced midwife. I happen to know this, as the same midwife, Nurse Skuse, delivered my younger brother Ben some five years later. My middle brother, Michael, was born in Trowbridge Hospital, which had a maternity wing.

Downside was quite an impressive three-bedroom house which my father had had designed for him by Frank Alford, an architect and the husband of his sister Maud. Frank had a business in Westbury where he made fireplaces. Downside was quite spacious, and needed a lot of heating. Initially there was no central heating, only coal fires in each room, including the bedrooms. In cold weather we used to huddle round the fire in the breakfast room. Sometime later central heating was installed by Geo Applegate and Son of Trowbridge. The house had a massive entrance hall, rather excessive in my view, (cold!) which featured an extravagant staircase (good for sliding down the rails!)

The house was, compared with others on the Down, quite large and Mother needed, and usually had, some help. Washing the clothes was done in some sort of machine tub with no spinner. To get most of the water out an attached wringer with exposed cogs was used. When I was 18 months old I put my left thumb into the cogs and promptly lost the top of it. Health and safety was unheard of at that time. Nowadays it would have been sown back on. I haven't forgotten it - how could I!

Alfie Crease, who owned the Wyke Brickworks in Canal Road, Trowbridge, called at Downside one day to see Father about his horse, Tickity, and I, aged about four, answered the door. On my damaged thumb was a large wart which Alfie spotted. He said 'I'll give you a penny for your wart'. I accepted the offer and within a day or so my wart was gone, and I have never had one since!

Apart from this, I and my two brothers had a very happy childhood. I do remember chasing around the lawn pushing the pram with my youngest brother Ben in it. Once it tipped over. Luckily Ben was strapped in and came to no harm. This demonstrated the value of seat belts, not invented at that time.

Percy Brunt at Catcombe Farm Hilmarton, with the two Springer Spaniels, Ben and Judy. The right hand 'toadstool' is the one I crashed into!

At the age of four I stayed at Catcombe Farm, Hilmarton, with my uncle, Ralph Brunt. I took my trike with me and rode it down this path, promptly crashing into the toadstool at the bottom. I still have a scar to remind me.

In 1936, at about four years old, I went to a kindergarten. This was on a farm at Widbrook, Bradford on Avon. They had a large billy goat which knocked me over several times. I couldn't put up with the blasted goat and I refused to go after the first week! This was the first of nine schools which I attended. I must have had a good education!

A picnic on the way to Weymouth for the day, 1939. From left: John, age 7, Henry, Phyllis and Michael age 6.

When I was seven, WW2 was raging, Mother was unwell and Michael (who was six) and I were packed off as Boarders to the Westholm School in Andover. Later we both went to the village school in Hilperton, which was, in fact, quite good. The Headmaster, a Mr Pearson, made sure we knew our 3 Rs. Later still, Michael and I were weekly boarders at Lord Weymouth's Grammar School in Warminster. I also had a spell at the Trowbridge Convent where I took a dislike to the Nuns in their Black Habits!

Another short spell was at Cannings College in Bath, which necessitated a 12-mile train journey passing through the famous Box Tunnel. Often, after school, I swam in the old Victorian swimming baths. This was quite primitive and had been built at least 150 years previously. It used the same hot spring water as in the Roman Baths nearby. It has since been demolished and replaced by a very expensive spa with a rooftop pool.

The war certainly upset my early education! With some extra coaching, I passed the Eleven Plus and went to Dauntsey's School, West Lavington, near Devizes (see Chapter 5). This proved to be absolutely right for me and was followed up with a year at Lackham School of Agriculture at Lacock, near Chippenham (Chapter 6).

At the age of about 14 there is always a temptation for youngsters to smoke. Michael and I were no exceptions. I did try the odd one or two. Father smoked quite heavily, probably 30 to 40 per day. Later, he did manage to give it up, but he never refused a free one! He knew it was a bad habit and was anxious that my brothers and I didn't take it up, so he developed a plan which did the trick. He offered £100 each to the three of us if we did not smoke until we were 21. The offer was accepted and honoured and I gave it up at the age of 16. I have smoked the odd small cigar and even now, if I was offered a Havana cigar, it would be gratefully received, especially at Christmas! I am very pleased that smoking has been banned in public spaces. I hope it will be banned in cars too!

There being no TV, the family often had 'singsongs' around the piano. My mother was an excellent pianist. Father played the saxophone, sometimes at home but mostly in the Hilperton Village Band.

Henry and Phyllis Walden in 1949 with John, top left, Michael next to him and Ben in front on left holding Chaser, a Norwich terrier.

On the left is the rear of Halfway Cottage, Hilperton Road, Trowbridge, 1950. On the right is the rear of Downside, The Down, Trowbridge, circa 1938.

CHAPTER 3

LIFE ON A WILTSHIRE FARM, 1939-1942

I was very fortunate to have stayed many times at Manor Farm, Sandridge, near Melksham, which was farmed by Wilfred Giddings and his wife Hilda (née Brunt), plus their three children, my cousins, Mary, Gordon and Neville. The family had moved from Hoopers Pool Farm, Southwick, near Trowbridge to Manor Farm early in 1939.

Manor Farm covered 300 acres or more, mainly grassland. To begin with there was a herd of some 65 Shorthorn cows which were milked by hand, twice daily.

A milking machine was added by the time WW2 broke out. The milk was passed over a cooler into 10-gallon churns. Each morning it was collected by lorry and taken to Wiltshire United Dairies (WUD) in Melksham. WUD eventually became Unigate. Some time around 1942/43 the herd was wiped out by foot and mouth disease. This was a very sad and unpleasant occasion as all the carcasses had to be burnt. Once the all-clear was given a herd of British Friesians was established.

Wilfred Giddings was a big strong man. He needed to be! Everything was done by hand. Two shire horses, Bob and Colonel, provided the power. Tractors didn't come on the scene until about 1939. A Fordson was the first and then a Ford Major.

Animals at Manor Farm, Sandridge

A contented herd of Shorthorns similar to the ones at Manor Farm

A happy herd of British Friesian cows. Most of the UK's milk is produced from this breed.

A shire horse similar to Bob and Colonel, who were the 'workhorses' at Manor Farm (Bob and Colonel were black)

Just prior to the family moving into Manor Farm the farmhouse was very rudimentary. There was no shower or bathroom and a bath tub was still used. The toilets were across the yard near the dairy. These consisted of two seats, side by side above a 'thunderbox'. No toilet rolls, just newspaper. Not a place to linger in! This was also the case at Hoopers Pool Farm, Southwick, when the family left.

I am pleased to say that when I stayed there, a bathroom and toilet were in place and many improvements were made generally to make it a very comfortable home. The Giddings family always ate well and there was plenty of cream, especially on mashed potatoes! I was treated as one of the family and we all got on very well.

To begin with there was no mains water. Initially this had to be collected daily, both for the cattle and horses and the house. To get the water a horse and cart was used. When passable, the main source was about three quarters of a mile down Craters Lane (a rough grass track) or, when this supply dried up, on the hard road about a mile and a half away, where there was a stream. On one occasion, when I went with the carter, Reg Bray, we duly filled about six very large 17-gallon milk churns by bucket and set off back to the farm. Part way along Craters Lane there was a slight ditch crossing the lane. As we progressed through the ditch the horse had to give an extra pull and all the churns fell back over me and the carter. We were lucky not to have been hurt – we were just wet!

We had to go back for another load, otherwise, no water for the farm. No water, no milk, no income, no life! Fortunately around this time a moderately sized reservoir was constructed on the farm at the top of Sandridge Hill. This was a vast improvement and did the job until a connection was made to the mains water supply sometime in the early 1940s.

Apart from the family, three men were employed on the farm: Reg Bray, the carter, Bill Wilcox and Dennis Windel. Dennis, like Wilfred, was a well-built and powerful fellow, good fun and a good horseman. He rode in numerous point-to-point races, winning many of them. The family prospered at Manor Farm. A modern milking parlour was added and the Friesian dairy herd was increased. In due course, Gordon, who with JW also attended Dauntsey's School, took over from his father and added a thoroughbred stud, which was very successful. Neville branched out on his own and farmed at Watts Farm, Great Hinton, near Trowbridge (see Chapters 9, 15 and 17). Mary married Paul Stumbles, who was, for many years, a van salesman for Waldens.

CHAPTER 4

TROWBRIDGE BEFORE AND DURING WW2, 1938-1945

My recollections of Trowbridge in the late 1930s are that it was a busy and pleasant market town with a thriving weekly cattle market each Tuesday. The population would have been in the region of 11,000. The main employers were Wiltshire County Council, Trowbridge being the County town of the whole of Wiltshire including Swindon, which broke away around 2005. The impressive County Hall was built in the late 1930s.

Among the prominent businesses were Ushers' Wiltshire Brewery; Bowyers' pies and sausages; Chapman's mattress factory; Knees' department store (about the largest in Wiltshire at that time); Fear Hills, a smaller department store; Bert Pilkington's Model Laundry; F. Slugg, the printers; Frank Colborne, the jewellers; Aplins, the chemist; Wilkins and Darkins, men's clothes and Houlton's, photographers. Case and Sons, in Mortimer Street, were Bacon curers and produced super Hams for Christmas! Jack Case was the MD. Later, Cases moved to Martock in Somerset. There was a jolly good bike shop which sold Raleigh bikes, while Ernie Dennis was a Ford main dealer. Knees also had a removal business and a garage, and Jim Brindley was Garage Manager. There were Hiscock, engineers; Newman Hender, engineers; Applegates, central heating engineers; Drinkwaters, scrap metal merchants; Harrings, engineers; H R and S Sainsbury's, animal feed millers; Stone brothers, farmers and milkmen; Woolworths; Boots and W H Smith. We also had all the major banks, several of which have disappeared over the years. F. Slugg the printers supplied Waldens with food grade paper for wrapping butter. The owner when I dealt with Sluggs was John Culverhouse, ably assisted by Jim Nunn. There was a small, unattractive Co-op.

The veterinary surgeons were in Wingfield Road. The original partner was a Mr Golledge, followed by Dennis Archer and Messrs Parsons and Edwards. Dennis married the daughter of an estate agent, Phillip Snailam. Something went seriously wrong with this union and Dennis jumped off the roof of their house near West Ashton Road! Another prominent estate agent was Dennis Mugford.

The main hotel was the George. It had a nice ballroom and this often featured some famous musicians, including Hank Marvin and the Shadows, and Bert Weedon, the guitarist. I met my first girlfriend there, Valerie Fussell, daughter of Henry Fussell who owned the George and Fussell's Brewery in Rode. I often went shooting with Valerie's brother, Phillip, who was a crack shot.

There were many other smaller shops covering practically everything that a family needed. In general the people of Trowbridge were well served by its shopping centre without having to travel great distances. The nearest big city is, of course, Bath, and this was popular for a special day's shopping or a visit to the Theatre Royal. The Western National Bus Depot and the Great Western Railway ensured that Trowbridge wasn't isolated and was a good place in which to live and to do business.

Waldens, having grown out of the original factory, which was at the rear of the Lion and Fiddle Pub at Hilperton, had built the second one on the Down in 1928.

Earlier the prosperity of Trowbridge would largely have derived from the cloth industry. Around 1820 there were 20 cloth mills, making very high quality West of England worsted cloth, and Trowbridge was then known as the Manchester of the West. In the 1930s only seven remained, and these all closed down shortly after the end of WW2. Several of the buildings remain and now have different uses. The wool they used would have come from the thousands of sheep on nearby Salisbury Plain. In 1939 Army activities replaced the sheep and, one by one, the mills closed. At the same time a much faster method had been developed elsewhere and the local mills were unable to compete.

To maximise the army training area on Salisbury Plain, the entire village of Imber was cleared of all its inhabitants. In Trowbridge many of the mill owners' grand homes remain, particularly The Grange and Rodwell Hall in Victoria Road, Fieldways and several others in Hilperton Road.

There were three cinemas and the quite majestic town hall, which served as a centre for public meetings and entertainment, mainly dances. It also housed the local court. At the rear of the town hall there was an extensive park with a children's play area which had a brilliant roundabout. Some distance away there was a jolly good open air swimming pool which was built in about 1938. This is where my middle brother Michael and I learnt to swim. We began in April when the temperatures both in and out of the water were noticeably very cool. I have fond memories of the brilliant swimming instructor, whose name was Jock Burns. This super pool has since been demolished to make room for the massive Tesco supermarket.

An early picture of Trowbridge Town Hall. The large Market Hall is on the right and the Tuesday Cattle Market was behind it.

A notable character who lived in Hilperton road was Norman Pike. Apart from being a farmer at Manor Farm in Hilperton he was a very prominent and honest (as far as I know!) cattle dealer. At Ladydown, by the River Biss, there was an animal Feed mill run by Tommy Tucker, who lived with his wife Hazel in Victoria Road.

At the bottom of Castle Street, alongside and on the right of the River Biss, was the original Chapman Mattress factory, founded in 1871 by Hedley Chapman. Their first mattresses were packed with straw and called 'palliasses'. Later they were using by-products from the local woollen mills. In the 1950s the boss of Chapman's was John Yates. Around this time they had a major strike. Rather than give in to the excessive demands, which the company couldn't afford, John Yates closed the factory, locked the workers out and sacked them. Very quickly the worker's sensibly caved in, and production was re-started and expanded rapidly. The trouble makers were not reinstated.

Chapman's mattress factory at Cradle Bridge, circa 1871 to 1950. Later to be known as Airsprung and moved to Ladydown.

The company's name was changed to Airsprung and soon it needed a larger modern factory. Waldens sold the firm the land at Ladydown, where Airsprung are prospering to this day.

Trowbridge had a good hospital, as well as a separate isolation unit where my brother Michael spent about a month with scarlet fever. Visitors could only look through the window when they went to see him in his small cubicle. He was lucky to survive. I had a number of spells in Trowbridge Hospital due to abscesses on my neck, which kept appearing and needed removal. I understand that these were due to bacteria present in unpasteurised milk. Luckily there were some good doctors, particularly Dr Roger Wright, who attended the Walden family.

Prior to WW2 there was a WW1 tank on display in the park. When the Second World War started this was removed, together with all the iron fences which were scattered all over the town. This was all recycled to be turned into guns and tanks.

Early in the war two large purpose-built factories were erected to produce Spitfires in vast numbers. Many of the parts were made by local engineers in the town, including Harrings in West Street off Wingfield Road. Parts were assembled in a building in Hilperton Road, opposite Victoria Road. Once the main components of the planes (wings and main body) were completed in the two factories they were transported on some massive trucks, known as Queen Marys, to a large aircraft hangar on Keevil Airfield. Separately the engines would arrive from Rolls Royce at Filton, near Bristol and once installed they would be flown, mainly by women pilots, to wherever they were needed.

Members of the ATA (Air Transport Auxiliary) who would have flown the Spitfires from Keevil Airfield to wherever they were needed.

Thousands of Spitfires, like this one, were built in Trowbridge without the attention of the Luftwaffe. If we hadn't had the Spitfire and the brave "Few" who flew them, the Battle of Britain would have been lost. Hitler would have walked over us and where would be now? It doesn't bear thinking about!

Hiscocks were prominent engineers going back several generations. Prior to the war they invented and made egg grading machines. The design was sold to Newman Hender, also in Trowbridge, who marketed them as Ben Nevis egg grading machines and sold them worldwide. These were used by Waldens.

At Ladydown, at the bottom of Canal Road, Alfie Grease had his brickworks with its extensive clay pit, much of which was full of water. For the Walden family, who lived on The Down, milk was delivered by horse and cart and the farmer, Wilfred Stone, from Wyke Farm near Hilperton, served the milk direct from churns into the householder's milk cans. Not particularly hygienic! I remember that, on Wilfred and Cecil Stone's farm, the elevator they used to lift hay on to a hayrick or into a barn was driven by a pony continually walking round and round.

A couple of other things I recall. One is the regular visits in the summer of the Walls Ice Cream man. He came on a trike with his ice cream in a large container in the front. This unit was known as 'the stop

me and buy one' No special offers like 'Buy one and get one free'! The other thing was that gipsies called regularly trying to sell clothes pegs they had made. They were much bigger and clumsier than the ones in use today.

The Walls Ice Cream "Stop me and buy one" trike with a container on the front was a regular visitor.

Trowbridge had a very special parish church and several schools; one was Trowbridge High School (one for boys and one for girls). Another was Nelson Haden and another was a convent. Crime was minimal in the area and Chief Superintendent Hector Shears in the modern police station in Polebarn Road kept it under strict control. The local blacksmith shod horses next to Bowyers' sausage factory. He was a Mr Wrintmore and he shod our horse, Wendy. Having spent many years shoeing horses the poor fellow was constantly bent almost double.

There was also a small college in Hill Street, where those who had left school could extend their studies. I was one. I learnt to type! You could possibly also learn shorthand there, as this was invented by Sir Isaac Pitman, who was born in Trowbridge. The museum in Trowbridge is well worth a visit, as are the ones at Devizes and Calne.

Like most towns Trowbridge had a rugby, football and cricket team, each having their dedicated playing fields. There was a large army barracks where the Wiltshire Regiment or Wiltshire Yeomanry would have been based and, as horses were still in use by the army, there was extensive stabling. (My father bought a 'retired' war horse from the barracks – see Chapter 16.) Soldiers who were based in Trowbridge would have trained on Salisbury Plain, where they would sleep in tents and their horses would be tied up in lines close by.

As WW2 approached the army quickly became mechanized and horses were gradually phased out. Bren gun carriers were a regular feature. One, I remember, went completely out of control in Victoria Road at the crossroads with St Thomas's Roads and Middle Lane. It went round and round in circles at least ten times, tearing up the tarmac, before the driver managed to regain control.

The number of troops in and around Trowbridge rapidly increased, to the extent that many were billeted on local families. Waldens' factory, which by 1939 was well established as manufacturers of meat pies, were prominent in supplying the troops over a wide area and this certainly helped towards making the business prosper.

In 1943, when preparations had begun for the invasion of Europe, thousands of American GIs descended upon Trowbridge. They built a large camp off Bradley road, where Wiltshire College is now established. All the Trowbridge lads were already 'doing their bit' and had left the girls behind. The GIs in their smart uniforms and with bulging wallets were given a great welcome by the local lasses and my brother and I had to do our best to turn a blind eye to their amorous activities!

The River Biss, a tributary of the Bristol Avon, runs through the town. This was subject to regular flooding. I recall that on one occasion, when I was about seven years old, the flood was quite bad, but I attempted to ride through it on my bike. Part way across it was about three feet deep. Luckily someone came to my rescue. The River Avon at Staverton regularly flooded over a wide area. It was often worse at Bradford on Avon, where it could be impassable. The only way of getting to and from Bath was via a viaduct at Avoncliffe which took the Kennet and Avon Canal over the river. The canal is on the edge of Trowbridge, at Ladydown, and with the River Avon, it was just right for fishing and canoeing. Horse-drawn barges were still in use on the canal, and these were mainly to carry coal from the Somerset coalfields in the Radstock area. Coal was the main source of power for the cloth mills in Trowbridge. It was also the prime source of power for producing steam in the Waldens' factory.

About four miles from Trowbridge is Farleigh Hungerford, with its medieval castle, which has its own dungeon. Below the castle runs the River Frome. This has a super pool above a Weir which was, and is, ideal for unrestricted 'wild swimming'. Once Michael and I could ride our bikes on the Highway we made good use of it. It had a springboard for diving. The area around Trowbridge was very rural with many medium-size family farms, mainly engaged in producing milk. This would have been collected daily in churns and taken to Wilts United Dairies in Melksham. The head office for the dairies was in Hilperton Road,

Trowbridge, and in time this became Unigate. Trowbridge was, indeed, the centre of the dairy Industry.

At the outbreak of war the village of Keevil, about five miles from Trowbridge, was selected to build an airfield to be used for the planes and gliders which took many of the paratroopers to Arnhem. It was also the main base for hundreds of new Spitfires which were built in Trowbridge. Many SOE personnel were flown from Keevil to link up with the French and Dutch resistance behind enemy lines. Trowbridge helped win the war in more ways than one!

There is some beautiful country around Trowbridge which should be visited. Bowden Hill, Lacock, is very special, as is the Westbury White Horse and Bowood House near Calne. As a point of interest there are eight white horses in Wiltshire. The eighth was made to commemorate the millennium just north of Devizes, on the side of Roundway Down. This is close to the site of a major victory by the Royalists in the English Civil War in 1643 (see www.devizesheritage.org.uk). In about 2000, during a walk over the Downs, I and my family picked up dozens of round bullets and larger cannonballs which had recently been uncovered when the field was ploughed. Many of the local villages are worth a visit and the Avon valley between Bradford-on-Avon and Bath is particularly beautiful. The Trowbridge Museum is exceptional, see www.trowbridgemuseum.co.uk

When war broke out, I would have been about seven years old – old enough to realize what was happening, both locally and around the world. There was no TV and the Walden family closely followed events by listening to the radio and reading the *Daily Telegraph*. Even at my young age, I was well aware of what Hitler was up to. Once he was made Chancellor of Germany and Austria in 1933 he set about re-arming Germany as fast as possible. His intention was to conquer the whole of Europe, including the UK. He invaded Russia, which was his downfall, and that was the turning point in the Allies' favour. One of the main reasons for his failure on the Eastern Front, as it was called, was the ferocious Russian winter.

Many readers will know that the Prime Minister at that time was Neville Chamberlain and he tried to form a pact with Hitler which he thought would persuade him not to invade the UK. Chamberlain was at the very least naïve and was completely taken in by Adolf. He came home from a meeting with the Führer proudly announcing that he had made peace with Germany.

Like the German youth, Chamberlain was taken in by the cunning and ruthless Herr Hitler, who had no intention of honouring this agreement. There were several UK politicians who held similar views to Chamberlain. Fortunately one man in particular had the foresight to see through Hitler's dishonesty and Chamberlain's ineptitude and stupidity. He was, of course, Winston Spencer Churchill.

The people of the United Kingdom owe Winston more than any other statesman. Against massive opposition, Churchill continually advocated, even before 1938, that the UK should make preparations to meet Hitler head on. Luckily for us all, Winston's views prevailed. He won the argument and later the war. Had Hitler invaded the UK it is on record that he planned to have all males castrated to ensure the dominance of the Germanic

Winston Spencer Churchill. An exceptionally great man.

race. I'm extremely glad that I was spared this! I understand that he didn't bomb Oxford as he intended to make that City his HQ, if he had conquered the UK.

We all know that without the very considerable help Europe received from the USA we would now be under the evil control of the Nazis, a fate which does not bear thinking about. Fortunately Winston had some close connections 'over the pond'. His mother, Lady Randolph Churchill, was American and Winston had a good rapport with the then President of the United States of America, Franklin D Roosevelt. At this time the American public were very much anti-war. They took the view that the war in Europe was our problem and had nothing to do with them. Roosevelt had to take note of this if he was to survive and win the next presidential election. Personally, however, he did support the British cause, and instead of sending troops he agreed to ship masses of vital arms, food and equipment. America also began to build hundreds of 'Liberty Ships' with which to carry the cargoes. These mass-produced ships were also produced in the UK and Canada and their contribution towards winning the war was immense. Without them we would have starved.

It took the Japanese raid on Pearl Harbour, which sank the greater part of the American battle fleet, to persuade the American Public that WW2 was theirs as well as ours. The war against the Japanese was as ferocious as the war in Europe and it is worth recording for future generations, who I hope will read this book, that the Americans brought the war in the Pacific to an abrupt end by dropping atomic bombs on Japan. This saved many lives.

The war in Europe was bloody, to say the least. On a visit to Normandy in France in 2008, I was taken by some French friends, Mokhtar and Delphine Lance, to an American War Cemetery. There were 10,000 US troops laid to rest there and many had been killed on the first day of the D-Day landings on Omaha Beach. We must never forget the debt we owe to all who made sure WW2 was won by the Allies.

On the home front in Trowbridge during WW2, hundreds of Spitfires were being made in two specially-built factories and three smaller ones in and around the town. Luckily the German Luftwaffe either didn't know about this or were not interested. They concentrated their activities in trying to flatten Bath and Bristol. From their point of view, they made a good job of it. The Blitz of Bath in WW2 was made into a documentary and was shown on the Yesterday TV channel in 2014. It is called the 'Baedeker Blitz' – Baedeker was a European tourist guide and, apparently the Germans used the city plans to plan their raids!

JW with Delphine Lance at the cemetery in Normandy

The Germans used a radio beacon direct from Cherbourg to Bath, which passed right over Downside, the Down, Trowbridge and the Anderson air raid shelter we were using. The raids were mainly on the 25th and 26th April 1942, both at night and in daylight. Bristol's raids followed on and were equally bad, if not worse, followed by Cardiff. I think this radio beacon was used for all three. Eventually Bletchley Park code breakers broke the German code and caused the German pilots to go off course. However, in the case of Bath and Bristol the pilots were able to follow the River Avon, which took them to their targets.

During these air raids the RAF, which was based at Colerne, near Bath, were kept busy day and night. (See Chapter 17 re John Trigg) Frequently we were able to watch dogfights between aircraft. I particularly remember watching one in daylight as Michael and I were walking back from Hilperton Village School. One German plane was shot down and the pilot bailed out. Members of the Home Guard, which included Henry, were kept busy rounding up odd pilots.

At night we tried to sleep in the Anderson shelter, but at the height of the raids we got on top and had a bird's eye view of the raids on Bath and Bristol, where a large number of people lost their lives. As the hundreds of German bombers passed overhead we knew there was a raid on, as their engine noise was easily distinguished from British aircraft. In fact, it was quite frightening! Only three bombs fell on Trowbridge and these would have been dropped by bombers being chased by Spitfires so that they could lighten their load and go faster. One flattened a popular pub and two others destroyed houses. A fourth hit the bank of the Kennet and Avon Canal, letting all the water out as well as the fish. Three innocent cows were killed close by.

Until now, I had thought the Market Tavern, which was the favourite of the local farming fraternity and my father Henry, was the pub which had been destroyed. On a recent visit to Trowbridge Museum, where I met the prominent Trowbridge historian Roger Newman, I established that this was not the case. Apparently it was the Bear. Among the prominent farmers who regularly patronised the Market Tavern and escaped the bombing that night would have been Charlie, Tom and Jack Tucker and Don Banwell. Gordon 'Bud' Tucker and Jim Oram, sons of farmers, were already on active service, Bud in the Army and Jim a Lancaster Bomber pilot. Much later I recall enjoying a pint or two with Henry and brother Michael in the Market Tavern. Michael remembered that the jovial and popular landlord was Mark Bagnall.

After the war, while on the subject of drinking, several of us youngsters, including Gordon and Neville Giddings, regularly met at the King Arms in Melksham and, I am sure, consumed more pints of 'Green Label' than was good for us. Luckily the breathalyser had not yet been invented!

Early in the war a 'British Restaurant' was built in Trowbridge –

these restaurants were provided to ensure that everyone had a square meal. The Ministry of Agriculture, under the Minister, farmer Hudson (later Lord Hudson) from Manningford, near Pewsey, decreed that all counties had to organize a War Agriculture Executive Committee, known as 'The War Ag'. This organisation was set up to ensure that all farmers produced as much food as possible. Any farmer who didn't come up to scratch could be removed from their farm. Without this the population would have starved and the war would have been lost. Rationing was very strict.

As a matter of interest, the Chairman of the Wiltshire War Agriculture Executive Committee was farmer Richard Stratton, of Longbridge Deverill, near Warminster

Lord Hudson, a very good Minister of Agriculture in WW2

Richard Stratton, Chairman of the Wiltshire War Agriculture Committee during WW2

In the chapter (10) describing the development of Waldens of Trowbridge 1961 to 2005, I mentioned Ruth Cotton. Richard Stratton was Ruth's father. Ruth was instrumental in persuading me to begin the manufacture of frozen meals on wheels. I believe the man in charge of the local War Ag in Trowbridge was Bill Brimacombe. W T Price was the Chief Executive. Later Bill Price was appointed the Principal of Harper Adams Agriculture College in Shropshire.

Many British cities were heavily bombed in addition to London, notably Coventry. I can fully understand the thinking of Air Chief Marshal 'Bomber' Harris when he organised 1000 Bomber raids on Germany. No doubt this helped to shorten the war. He was criticised, quite wrongly, in my view, by Winston Churchill and it is only recently that a memorial has been erected in London to honour our many brave airmen who didn't return. We should not forget who started the war. At the same time we should spare a thought for the people of Berlin and Dresden whose cities were devastated, like the many British cities which were targeted.

We owe a great debt to the RAF. Two of my relatives, cousins Percy Brunt, a Mosquito Pathfinder Pilot (See Chapter 17) and John Trigg, who married my cousin Norah Brunt both, played their part. John flew Mosquitoes from Colerne during the raids on Bath and Bristol. Thousands gave their lives so that we and future generations can enjoy our freedom. We should of course recognise all servicemen and women who made sure we won the war, as well as those who kept the home fires burning and backed them up. Other members of the Brunt family also did their bit in WW2. (See Chapter 17).

CHAPTER 5

BOARDING SCHOOLS, 1939–1949

Early in WW2 my mother Phyllis Harriet (her nickname as a child was Pee) developed a nasty problem with a thyroid gland. She had difficulty in coping with her two boisterous sons, me and Michael. It was decided that the best solution was to pack us both off to boarding school. The chosen destination was Westholm School, The Avenue, Andover, Hampshire, about 30 miles from Trowbridge. I was seven and Michael six. Another pupil at the school was John Tarrant, a farmer's son who lived at Castle Farm, Over Wallop, near Andover. Later we were to meet again at Dauntsey's and we have been great friends ever since.

What influenced the choice was the fact that one of Henry's sisters, my Aunt Margery, lived on The Avenue close to the school. Marge's husband, Arthur, was a van salesman for Waldens and Andover was his base. He was one of the fortunate ones who survived WW1, although he lost a kidney through enemy action.

Michael and I settled in to Westholm School with considerable misgivings. It wasn't the best period of my life! The Headmaster, a Mr Caldecott, was a bit of a sadist and took pleasure in beating Michael for the slightest infringement of school rules, which he appeared to make up as he went along. His wife, who was also the Matron, was, on the other hand, not only very pleasant but also very attractive. Last thing at night she would check the dormitory to make sure that all was well and that no one had absconded! (I forget how many boarders were at the school - very few, I suspect.) This proved to be one of the highlights of our short period at Westholm as she would insist in wearing a see-through nightie! At this stage of our education Michael and I hadn't had the opportunity to learn about the 'birds and the bees' but we were well aware of, and appreciated, the beauty of the opposite sex. It was our introduction to this interesting subject, and never to be forgotten. It does come naturally!

Much later we were on holiday in Weymouth and John Tarrant, with his sister Margaret and mother Mary, happened to be on holiday in the same hotel at the same time. We had a day trip by boat to Jersey. It was a very rough crossing and most passengers were violently seasick. Apart from that it was fine!

Each Friday after lunch, Arthur Seymour, our uncle, parked his fair-sized van outside his house in The Avenue about

Mother (Phyllis) with Mary Tarrant on the promenade at Weymouth, 1948

75 yards from Westholm School. We took careful note of his movements, as we had an ulterior motive. At about 2 pm he would set off for Trowbridge, where he would replenish his stock of the wide variety of products which Waldens made. He would then return to Andover with a full load in readiness for the following week's business.

After a couple of weeks, Michael and I were planning the best means of escape. It wasn't difficult. We knew when Uncle Arthur would be leaving for Trowbridge and we quickly decided that this was the answer to our prayers. It would be quite easy, no security fence to climb and no tunnel to dig. When the coast was clear we just walked out of the front gate of the school and casually walked down the road and climbed into the back of the van. Arthur had no idea that he was carrying an 'illegal' cargo, and he drove to Trowbridge with all speed. We did this at least twice and our father got a bit cross, having to drive us back to Andover when petrol was very scarce and rationed.

On one of the trips to Andover the road was very icy and we had to negotiate the very dangerous left-hand bend at the bottom of the hill as you leave Upavon on the way to Andover, passing RAF Upavon, as it was then. The bend was covered in lethal black ice and the camber, like many roads at that time, was in the wrong direction. The Austin Princess Father was driving spun round in a full circle. No damage was done and no one hurt, and we were soon back at Westholm under much tighter security. I know that once the dust had settled we escaped a second time. Shortly afterwards Father removed us from the school altogether. We didn't shed any tears!

Lord Weymouth's school, Warminster 1943

Michael and I went as weekly boarders to Lord Weymouth's school, I think for one year. It was, one of nine schools I attended and quite good when compared with many of the others. Among the illustrious pupils, apart from Michael and me, were two Thynne brothers. The elder, somewhat eccentric one is now Lord Bath, who is at the helm at Longleat. I am reminded that the Headmaster was Mr Macdonald. I am sure he was very good, although my memories of my time at Lord Weymouth's are few and somewhat dubious!

We were introduced to games and I especially recall cross-country running over some terrible rough and boggy tracks. The school's second master was a Mr Charlton and the geography teacher was a particularly beautiful young, golden-haired woman, about 25 years old. While we were there, they became engaged. Had I been of a similar age, Mr Charlton wouldn't have stood a chance; lucky Mr Charlton!

On one hot and beautiful summer's day, I, with about 25 other pupils, attended a geography lesson on the lawn at the rear of the school. Our teacher was this auburn beauty. We gathered around sitting on the dry lawn with the teacher sitting in front of us on a chair. I was sitting next to a randy fellow called Wilmot. At this stage I was about 11 years old and had only a very rudimentary knowledge of the birds and bees – this subject would not be on the school curriculum until some seventy years later. Suddenly, Wilmot gave me sharp nudge, diverting my attention from the lesson in hand. He pointed out that the dear girl had omitted to put on a vital item of underwear. I understand that 50 years ago it was quite normal for women not to wear knickers! I do not recall the content of this lesson or any others at Lord Weymouth's school – I wonder why? But I'm sure I did learn some things that were useful.

Another highlight of my spell at Lord Weymouth's was the visit of Queen Mary, the wife of King George V, to Warminster. Warminster was important as it was, and still is, a 'garrison' town with close proximity to the military training area on Salisbury Plain. I think the whole school lined the street to see her. This would have been about 1943.

An imposing portrait of Lord Weymouth's Headmaster, Ian P MacDonald MA, 1940 to 1958 (PS I can't remember him!)

The 'Wren' door at Lord Weymouth's School. This door was originally designed by Sir Christopher Wren as the front door to Longleat House. It is believed that it was moved to the school in 1662 when a new door was commissioned by Sir James Thynne of Longleat, prior to the visit of King Charles II and Queen Charlotte in 1663. It must have been well made as it still in place today, over 500 years later. (I am indebted to Geraldine Frankling, the current Receptionist of Warminster School, for this information.)

Dauntsey's School, 1945 to 1949

I was very fortunate at the age of thirteen to go to Dauntsey's School, West Lavington, near Devizes, in January 1945. WW2 was still raging but Dauntsey's was well away from the action. All new Boarders were accommodated at the Manor House set in some lovely grounds about 2 miles from the main school. This meant that we had to walk through the woods, in all weathers, to attend our lessons. Quite often we arrived wet through. At this time the uniform, until you were in the Upper Sixth Form, included shorts whatever the weather and in 1947 it was extremely difficult to protect your most vulnerable body parts.

Dauntsey's School Manor House, originally the home of the Pleydell-Bouverie family

The Manor House Sanatorium at Dauntsey's, 1947

Life at the Manor was pretty good in spite of the very strict food rationing. To supplement my rations, I recall bringing large quantities of beef dripping from home which I spread on bread. Beef in those days had considerably more fat than it does today. The main school had a tuck shop which provided a regular supply of gorgeous cream buns!

The Manor House was quite extensive and there were large cellars under the greater part of the house. They were, of course, out of bounds, but a number of us found means of entering them, which was quite exciting. Some boys used it to have an uninterrupted smoke, but not me! I understand that the cellars were later used as locker rooms for the Pupils.

One of the pupils I met soon after I arrived was John Tarrant, who had been at Westholm School, Andover. Our friendship blossomed and several times I stayed with John on his farm at Over Wallop in Hampshire, which was great fun. I remember we shot a lot of rooks on the annual rook shooting day, the 12th of May. Sadly, John's dad died when he was about 15 and he left Dauntsey's to help his mum run the farm. John became a very good farmer and later I was able to buy a lot of super turkeys and capons from him.

The future Farmer Tarrant, age 16. John's first venture into poultry, rearing point-of-lay pullets.

View of Castle Farm, John checking his Friesian Cows

Driving the tractor.

On one side of the Manor House is a steep bank which forms the side of a valley through which runs a stream. Sometime before I went to Dauntsey's, a super swimming pool had been built using the water from the stream, which in those days was quite clear and free of pollution, something which was almost unknown then. As soon as we went back to school for the summer term we began swimming in this unheated pool. To begin with it was so cold that your skin turned blue! Each pupil had to prepare for a swimming proficiency test. I passed this and it stood me in good stead for my future waterborne activities, canoeing and sailing.

The super swimming pool in the valley at Dauntsey's Manor House. In the top picture, note the springboard on the right. This pool was later filled in. I am sure it could have been saved, and should have been.

In the exceptionally cold winter of 1947, when temperatures dropped to -20 C, the school heating system was totally inadequate. To keep warm it was necessary to huddle up around the radiators. Food was still rationed and, to make things worse, vegetables were in very short supply because of the continuous hard frosts. Potatoes couldn't be stored without being ruined by the frost. The whole school, 300 boys plus the staff, had lunch in the spacious dining hall. The masters sat at the top table, which was at a higher level. This enabled George Olive, the Headmaster, to keep a strict eye on what was going on. His eyes must have been good, as he spotted my plate and noticed that I wasn't eating my potatoes. He promptly left his seat and made a beeline for me.

'Walden!' he said, 'why aren't you eating your potatoes?' To which I responded that they were inedible. And so they were. He accepted my answer. I'm sure he looked into the problem, as we did get better spuds afterwards.

To provide a respite from the atrocious weather, one of the worst winters ever recorded, probably worse than 1963, a snowball fight was organized, Manor House v the main school. The Manor boys had the advantage of being on top of the hill above the swimming pool and the main school boys were pelted relentlessly as they tried to climb the steep hill. I'm not sure who won, but it was great fun.

Each morning at the main school we had to assemble in the Farmer Hall. The Headmaster addressed the 300-odd boys making any special announcements and singling out any pupil who he wished to report to his study. One day I was the subject of his attention; he accused me of using my bike, which in Form 4 was banned. He had forgotten that only a week before he had given me special dispensation to have my bike at school. My doctor had recommended that I cycle as much as possible to try and strengthen my ankle, which had been severely damaged playing rugby and in the gym. Sixty-seven years later it is still a problem. As my home in Trowbridge was only 14 miles away I often cycled there at a weekend making sure I was back in time for supper. Escapology was becoming a habit!

After the first year at Dauntsey's we were moved to the main school. This had a continuous passage the full length of the building, pretty well 100 yards. When my ankle was in good shape two of my friends (John Griffiths and David Walter) and I used to play 'touch' up and down the corridor. On one occasion as I was running flat out, Mr Olive walked out at a junction and he and I collided. Unintentionally I knocked him down. He saw red, and when he got to his feet he gave me a sharp slap across the face. This activity was banned, with immediate effect.

Even after this episode I still held him in great respect. I noticed, much later, that the corridor had been sectioned off, probably as a fire precaution. It was great fun while it lasted!

One of the masters at that time was a Frenchman, Harry Ault. Not a nice Frenchman. He excelled at dishing out 'lines' by the hundred and

The impressive front of Dauntsey's School

I collected many of them. In my early days at Dauntsey's I was a bit of a rebel and didn't knuckle down to my studies. Consequently I was often in trouble and with a few others had to report to the Headmaster at regular intervals, usually on a Monday morning after assembly. It was a bit of disgrace to have to line up waiting to go into his study. George would, at the least, give me a good dressing down and if my misdemeanours were serious he would use the cane. This went on for nearly a year and I eventually got fed up with it. In the end I decided it was time I pulled my socks up. I wish I had done so earlier. Better late than never!

The gymnasium at Dauntsey's was especially good and we had two very fine gym masters. The senior one was Captain Keen, a veteran of WW1, who was exceptional. Sometime after WW2 had ended he was joined by 'Killer' Norris, an ex-army Lieutenant, PT instructor. I was reasonably good in the gym. Norris was in fact a very pleasant chap and a first-class PT instructor. One of his exercises was swinging a heavy weight round a circle of pupils, and as it came to each one you had to jump it. On one occasion I got the timing wrong and was knocked off my feet, fell and broke my wrist. I think this exercise was discontinued after this accident. Quite right too!

Until some time after the war, the teaching staff consisted of many older people, men and women. I particularly remember Miss Arnold, who did her best to teach me Latin, and the Rev Joe Jenkins, who taught me Maths in Form 4. To his amazement, mine and many others, I managed to get 100% in the end-of-year Maths exam. I think I must have taken it easy after that. Another Maths master we had was E R B Reynolds. This teacher was obviously quite clever. The only trouble was he expected his pupils to know the subject before we started and then he went ahead at such a rate it was impossible to take it all in. I gave up! A complete opposite was George Olive, who taught me general science. George was brilliant!

The excellent first gymnasium, later demolished

Back row (those I remember): 2nd from left ALB Canham, Stephen Brown, Peter Moody, and Geoffrey Gotch. Front row: 3rd from left Jim Pickford, Captain Keen.

Other teachers I particularly remember were John Scott, who taught English and was the master in charge of the Manor House, and E L B Batten, who taught Engineering Design and was very good. I managed to get a distinction in this subject in my School Certificate. I also

G W Olive, Lord Tedder and Col RW Awdry

Mr and Mrs G W Olive's Silver wedding 1945
Those I remember: Back row, 4th from left, I T 'Buttercup' Hamilton; 6th from left Mrs Jago; B W H
Coulson; 11th from left H C Ault, Mary Olive; 15th from left, Captain Keen. Middle row from left: Miss
Arnold, F N S Creek. 4th from left, ERB Reynolds, George Olive, Mrs Olive, E L B Batten. 2nd from
right: R S Barron.

remember F N S Creek, Geography and Cricket; 'Buttercup' Hamilton, Biology; J O Thomas, Agriculture; R S Barron, Physics; P A M Russell, Latin and Rugby; R N Venebles, Rugby; and F H Brown, History. Several of these teachers and others had just returned from the war. The school had a 'panel' of governors, part of whose duty was to ensure the school was run to well-established and proven standards. I am quite sure they had no trouble while George Olive was at the helm. One of the governors in my time at Dauntsey's was the Marshall of the Royal Air

Force, Lord Arthur Tedder. One of Lord Tedder's sons was a pupil there when I joined the school in January 1945.

I could run quite fast and in rugby I played on the wing. Mr Venebles, who instructed us, was much faster and had played rugby at international level. During one practice game he decided to demonstrate his prowess at tackling and used me for this purpose. I was running flat out for the line when suddenly, without warning, Venebles demonstrated a flying tackle. He took off and crashed straight into my back, knocking me flying. He would have been about 13 stone and I was less than 9. I was winded and needed a few minutes to recover, after which play was resumed.

Anyone who was educated during the war was at a definite disadvantage, as most of the best teachers were called up for military service. It was several years before things returned to normal. I have no doubt that it affected my education. That's my excuse and I am sticking to it!

Dauntsey's, which was founded in 1542, began as a school primarily for farmers' sons and this was largely the case when I was there. The school farm of some 40 acres had a milking herd, plus pigs and sheep. At this early stage of my life, it was my intention to become a farmer, so in the sixth form I chose to spend my time on the farm. J O Thomas had been in charge of the farm, but before I moved to the sixth form he had left to take up the post of the first Principal of Lackham school of Agriculture at Lacock. In his absence a Mr Marsden taught Agriculture. Mr Marsden was a nice man but was unable to keep order in his lessons, and pupils took advantage of this shortcoming. The Agriculture lessons were held in what was then the physics lab/classroom and Mr Marsden always brought his books to the class in a scruffy old brown case, which he plonked on the bench in front of the blackboard. I remember during one lesson some bright spark grabbed the case when his back was turned and quickly hid it from his view. Matters got completely out of hand.

Mr Marsden only lasted one term. A new master, Harry Adcock, was appointed and he was very good. Some years after George Olive had retired, the farm was disbanded. Much of the land has since been developed by the school, which is now one of the best-equipped schools in the UK and regularly performs well in the league tables. It is providing a good all-round education, something from which I most definitely benefited.

Bullying at Dauntsey's was quite rare. While I was there we were regularly fed Waldens' pies, which, although I am biased, were pretty good. One particular fellow by the name of Gaisford chose to tease me relentlessly over the contents of the pies, to the extent that one day I had had enough. I'm generally a fairly tolerant guy but this time, Gaisford provoked me too far. I let fly with a right hook straight on the nose and drew blood. He recovered, but he never teased me again. I expect today I would be charged with GBH!

In addition to the super playing fields in front of the main school, an additional playing field was added near the Manor House. This was known as the Warrington Field and it was largely used for athletics and field events. It had taken the best part of five years to prepare. I had a useful turn of foot. In the Fourth Form I competed in several field events, including the 400 yards, and broke the school junior record. My name was put up with all the other record holders, going back many years, in the gym, and I was quite proud of this.

Annually, the top athlete would be awarded the Nairn Cup in memory of a former outstanding pupil. Some years later the gym was demolished, I am not quite sure why, as it was very good, and the record board went with it. I was disgusted! I only held the record for one year before it was beaten by a fellow pupil Tim Bailey.

In rugby I managed to get a place in the Junior Colts, but a recurring ankle injury often disrupted this activity. I had boxing lessons under 'Killer' Norris and often sparred with John Meakin, who was a great friend. John was quite a bit taller than me and had much longer arms, so I didn't stand a chance. I dropped boxing quite soon, having decided that I preferred to retain my head in good working order. Helmets weren't worn in those days!

I played squash regularly, mostly with John Meakin, and we were evenly matched. Some years later John and I were at Lackham school of Agriculture together under J O Thomas, the Principal. Later still I married John's sister Ann.

In my time at Dauntsey's there were no girls. In the sixth form it was possible to have dancing lessons, which were held in the Farmer Hall. To overcome the absence of girls, a number were imported from Devizes, and one or two of them were very attractive. The school had a super library, which I made use of, and altogether Dauntsey's was quite special.

On Saturday evenings a film show was laid on in the Farmer Hall, and this was always very popular. Other pupils I especially remember are Roger Osborne, Peter Moody, Michael Noad, Richard Corp, Sam Gillett and John Coggan. Sam Gillett was a prefect and he gave me six of the best with a slipper for a minor infringement of the rules! Michael Noad and I were lucky enough to go the Olympic Games in London (White City I believe) in 1948, which was super.

There were excellent workshops for both Engineering and Woodwork, which I took advantage of. By and large I enjoyed my schooldays at Dauntsey's and they have stood me in good stead throughout my adult life. Looking back on my life I am sure that my time at Dauntsey's has had a great bearing on my success in everything I have done, especially business. I would like to record my thanks to all the staff who did their utmost to get the best out of me, especially George Olive. Unlike some public schools, which I know are very good, Dauntsey's produces adults who are able to mix with all walks of life and I hope it will continue to do so. Apart from General Science, which

George taught, one thing he mentioned which stands out in my memory was that when you fold a letter or any document, you should complete the fold to about a quarter of an inch short of the edge of the paper. This ensures that it can be opened easily by the recipient.

George Olive moved to a pleasant bungalow in Warminster when he retired and, some time later, I attended his funeral at Warminster Minster. The church was packed, which showed I wasn't the only one who had held him in great respect and fondness. George was an exceptionally good headmaster. Later ones, all of whom I have known, have not got near his qualities.

As a point of interest I understand that prior to WW2 in 1936 several exchange visits were made with German schools. Hitler, by then, had come to power and his disgusting influence was affecting all German youth. I believe that the pupils who went on the exchange trips were quite intimidated by the attitude of the Germans. I gather that up until that time many of the staff at Dauntsey's were pacifists. The outbreak of war must have changed their outlook and many of them joined the British forces and acquitted themselves exceptionally well. Most of them were fortunate to survive the war, as they returned to Dauntsey's and taught me!

During one summer holiday at the age of 16, I was fortunate enough to hire a cruiser on the Norfolk Broads with my brother Michael and two of his school friends. This proved to be quite an adventure. It was my first taste of being the skipper of a boat and definitely influenced my future activities afloat! I recommend it, not only for youngsters, but also for family holidays.

Long term, I kept in close touch with Dauntsey's and my three sons, Hugh, Sam and Joseph, were pupils. The younger one, Joseph, went on to Oxford Brookes and graduated with a BSc in Automotive Engineering. All three have benefited from their time at Dauntsey's.

CHAPTER 6

LACKHAM SCHOOL OF
AGRICULTURE, 1949-1950

After school I had a gap year during which I enjoyed my freedom, riding horses as much as possible. I looked after 10 rather special Wessex Saddleback Gilts (outdoors, using an electric fence) and milked the house cow. One highlight of this year was a holiday at Teignmouth with my friend Phillip Fussell, in their family caravan. Using a boat we concentrated on fishing for conger eels, and caught quite a number. The only problem was, what to do with them? I expect a celebrity chef would make good use of them. The stench from the ones we caught was diabolical, and we disposed of them as quickly as possible. It was a great holiday!

I reported to Lackham, at Lacock, near Chippenham in the autumn of 1949. Lackham had been established only the previous year with J O Thomas (ex Dauntsey's) as the first Principal. 'Jo' was the right man for the job, a 'round peg in a round ole'. The 100 students, who boarded full time, were a mixed bag. 50 of them were ex-servicemen who had recently been demobbed, ranging from privates and able seamen to officers. The other 50 were young fellows like me. It was a good mixture and we worked hard and played hard. Without exception, everyone was there to learn as much as possible, including JW!

The mature ex-servicemen element definitely had a favourable influence on the behaviour of the youngsters. Even in those days, when cars were relatively scarce, several of the students brought their own cars or motorbikes. John Meakin (ex Dauntsey's) had an Ariel 350cc. Having been 'born with a silver spoon in my mouth' (as someone mistakenly labelled me, many years later) I was lucky enough to have a second-hand MG TD which Father had bought from Knees' Garage in Trowbridge for £750, a lot of money in those days (see Chapter 16). Another student, Don Sturdey, had a motorbike and I rode on his pillion a few times, once skidding off the road and landing in a ditch full of cold muddy water. This put me off motorbikes for good. In future I kept to four wheels, or four legs! I also admired two pretty legs in nylon stockings!

Another student, Ivor Muggleton, arrived with an Allard car, which was quite impressive. I think his main objective was to impress the ladies. I am unsure as to whether he was successful!

Ivor Muggleton, and right, with his Allard K2. Quite a character!

Lackham House, 1946

J O Thomas, first Principal of Lackham School of Agriculture

JW, age 18

Jo Thomas had trained at Aberystwyth University, which was a major plant breeding centre. His speciality was grassland, and the pastures were his priority and main interest. High-producing leys were established and rotated and paddock grazing was practised. Farming was still labour intensive and mechanization was in its infancy. At the turn of the century a 300-acre farm would have employed about 12 workers. By 1950 the number would have been about six. In 2010 this would drop possibly to only two.

The farm was bounded by the River Avon on three sides. John Meakin, another good friend, John Pritchard, and I often swam from one end to the other, at least a mile, making sure we avoided a few fallen trees on the way. In addition to daily lectures, all the students took turns with the various enterprises on the farm, so that by the end of the year we were reasonably familiar with the essentials. It was a good preparation for the future. I was particularly interested in grassland, Jo Thomas's prime subject, and at the end of the course I came top. Whichever direction a student chooses to follow, the time spent at college or university is only the beginning. It is just an introduction, and you can expect to learn far more with practice, as I can confirm.

The main staff I remember at the college were Bill London, the Housemaster, Mr Nunn, a lecturer, Ted Witchell, engineering, Jack Chivers, the carter, Bert Stepney, who was in charge of the pigs, and Mr Hutchings, the woodman. The horses were still in regular use and I remember cutting and hauling mangolds on a very cold and frosty morning. This influenced my decision after completing my year at Lackham not to make farming my career. Farming was not ready for me, or I wasn't ready for farming!

The office staff were headed by a farmer's daughter, Joyce Guley, who was also Jo Thomas's Secretary. (I dated her once, nice but not naughty!) Joyce married Basil Richards, a Director of Unigate, and much later they farmed at Blackland Farm, Calne. Joe Thomas had a passion for Land Girls!

Lackham has an interesting collection of old tractors and machines. Ted Witchell, the engineering Instructor, in the driving seat, is helped by some students to get it going. JW is on the left (the good-looking one with the dark hair!) and Ivor Muggleton is on the right.

The Rugby 1st Team at Lackham. Top row: 4th from left, Don Sturdy, John E Meakin, Mr Nunn. Middle row: unknown. Bottom row: 3rd from left, John Walden, rest unknown

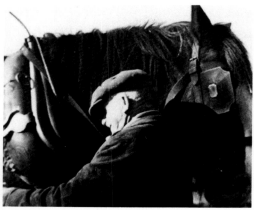

Jack Chivers with the last horse in use at Lackham. Later I was to use a pair of Percherons, harvesting on the Canadian prairie in Alberta (see Chapter 7).

There were only two courses to study, Agriculture in all its facets, and Horticulture. I chose Agriculture. There was a milking herd of 45 Friesians and a flock of some 100 Clun ewes. In addition there were extensive gardens and a large apple orchard. Three farms made up the total acreage, which included Cuckoo Bush on the road to Biddestone and one near Reybridge. As well as the Home Farm with the dairy, and the main house which was mainly used for boarding, there was a separate teaching block, which included a well-equipped workshop. During the latter part of WW2 American troops were based at Lackham. General Dwight Eisenhower used it as his HQ before moving to Southwick, near Portsmouth, where he and General Bernard Montgomery planned the D-Day landings in Normandy. The bathroom which Ike used still had a gold-plated handle which he had added. Ike, of course, after WW2 ended, became President of the USA.

In the next month or two, after the course had finished, John Pritchard and I took off in his Land Rover and headed for the west coast of Scotland. We camped in an ex US Army bivouac with one end open. When it was too wet we put it up under a barn! Another ex-student had settled on a croft on the west coast and we paid him a visit to get a taste of life as a crofter. A tough one, but lovely in the summer. If you camp in Scotland, be prepared for the midges! Later, John Pritchard immigrated to New Zealand, where he farmed deer. The antlers were exported to China, where they were valued for their aphrodisiac qualities.

All in all, my year at Lackham was very worthwhile, especially as my future business career was very closely tied to farming and farmers. Later, around 2002, my son Sam studied Countryside Management at Lackham, and this proved very valuable for him (see Chapter 12).

During the course of the year at Lackham we were fortunate enough to visit a number of establishments which were involved in, or connected, to agriculture. One was to the BOCM animal feed mill at Avonmouth. About 100 years previously the mill was sited at Avonmouth to deal with the vast quantities of maize, soya and ground nuts which were imported from North America and Africa. In 1950 the mill was very busy, but as things changed it soon closed. There were three farm visits, one to Jack Houghton Brown's Farm at Pertwood, south of Warminster, another to a farm at Stalbridge in Dorset, which was farmed by an ex-Lackham student (I believe his name was Benjafield), and the third to Arthur Hosier's Farm at Collingbourne Ducis, near Marlborough. Mr Hosier was the inventor and pioneer of the Hosier outdoor milking system using mobile milking parlours. This visit was especially interesting, and the system was one I would have considered adopting had I chosen to be a farmer. It would only be suitable on well-drained land to avoid excessive 'poaching'.

As I write these notes I have just made contact with a Hampshire farmer, Nick Snelgar, who is setting up the Hosier system to milk his herd of Jersey cows. I will follow his progress with interest. There is another very successful one in Devon.

Lackham was one of the best years in my quite eventful life, but by

Top: an original Hosier milking bail on Arthur Hosier's farm at Collingbourne Ducis

Right: modern Dutch milking bails

the time my year there came to an end I had changed my mind about farming as a career. Farming, at that time, was a very manual occupation, quite different to what it was to become 50 or 60 years later. However, some years later I did keep sheep and cattle. Farming is in my blood!

In 1950 conscription was still in force and it was mandatory from the age of 18 for all males to complete two years in the forces. Having decided that I no longer wished to be a farmer (which would have given me exemption), I was now liable to do my two years' National Service. Rather than two years I decided that I would do three, and signed on at the recruitment centre in Bath. The Korean War was at its height at that time and one of my school friends at Dauntsey's had been killed in action. My aim in joining up was mainly to have the chance of seeing the world, and three years would have given me plenty of opportunity.

However, when I got home my father persuaded me that my action in joining the army was not sensible. I agreed and rang the Recruiting Officer, and fortunately he cancelled my application. Although I didn't realize it at the time, I must have been destined to join the family business and use whatever talent I had in the food industry. The Walden family generally were not military material, although if things got a bit close I am sure they would rise to the occasion. My father did his stint in the Home Guard, rounding up German airmen who had parachuted after being shot down. Brother Michael did his National Service (see Chapter 17)

Just before this happened I was scanning through advertisements in the *Farmers' Weekly* when I spotted an advertisement which said 'See Canada, help needed with the harvest, passage out £10, return £15! I realised that this would be an ideal alternative to National Service. So it was that in 1951 I sailed for Canada.

CHAPTER 7

ACROSS THE ATLANTIC, 1951-52

I applied for the harvesting work at the Canadian High Commission in Cockspur Street, London. My application was accepted and in early May 1951 I boarded the Cunard liner M V *Georgic* (an ex WW2 troopship, now an immigrant ship) at Southampton and headed for Halifax, Nova Scotia.

From Southampton the *Georgic* headed for France, either Le Havre or Cherbourg. We dropped anchor and took on board a large number of passengers from various European countries. Quite a number of them had signed up on the same scheme as me, to help with the Canadian harvest. The second port of call was Cobh in southern Ireland, where quite a number of young Irishmen came aboard, either for harvesting or because they were making a new home in Canada. *Georgic* was being used to carry immigrants. Throughout WW2 the *Georgic* frequently carried as many as 3000 troops at the time, mainly from the USA and Canada to the UK. As she rolled very badly, having no stabilisers, it is easy to imagine the conditions on board when, in rough weather, the majority were seasick. Horrible!

On one particular voyage in the Mediterranean in 1943, near Suez, when she was transporting 1100 Italian POWs, she was bombed by the Luftwaffe. Her fuel caught fire and her ammunition magazine exploded. The mighty ship was burnt out and nearly sank. Somehow she was salvaged and towed back to Belfast where she had been built. In 1944 she was back in the war. When I travelled on her again in 1952 she was still in very good shape.

Cunard's RMS MV Georgic

I made a number of friends on the *Georgic* and in the evenings considerable quantities of Danish Carlsberg beer were consumed. In mid-Atlantic a violent storm developed, described by a member of the crew as possibly one of the worst storms a Cunard liner had ever experienced. The *Georgic* pressed on regardless and about a dozen of us stayed up late and enjoyed the Carlsberg. About three other Cunard ships 'hove to', but the *Georgic* passed them and pressed, rolling violently all the time. Stabilizers were unheard of at that time.

Around midnight all the Carlsberg drinkers retired to bed. I slept

The 'Carlsberg Brigade', the night before the storm. JW is behind the left hand corner of the table. Far right is a gentleman from Ireland. The rest are from Denmark, Holland, Belgium and Sweden.

well and, surprisingly, woke with a clear head. Next morning, when the storm was gradually dying, the situation in the ship generally was complete chaos, particularly in the dining room. 99% of the passengers were ill and didn't appear for breakfast, and most of the crew were laid low. Only one other passenger (from Belgium) came to breakfast and joined me. All the dining room furniture was scattered all over the floor. Luckily one chef and one steward were on duty. Both of us had a double Cunard breakfast, which was super!

After roughly five days at Sea, *Georgic* docked safely in Halifax, Nova Scotia. Halifax has an interesting history, as the Cunard Line was founded there in about 1839 by Samuel Cunard. Initially his sailing ships carried mail between Canada, the USA and the UK before including passengers. They were known as Royal Mail Ships (RMS). I was fortunate to return to the UK aboard the RMS *Queen Elizabeth* from New York in 1952 and much later in 2007, I enjoyed a Mediterranean

Cruise on the QE2, which was a fantastic ship. The QE2 was about the optimum size for a liner. Later models are, in the main, far too big, and I have no wish to sail on any of them.

From Halifax I headed straight for Toronto in Ontario, by rail, a journey of some 1500 miles or more. The railway line followed the St Lawrence Seaway and passed below the Heights of Abraham, above Quebec near where General Wolf defeated the French. Admiral Lord Horatio Nelson also took part in these battles in the early part of his career. The journeys by train were included in the £10 passage outward and again for the return journey from Alberta to the UK for £15. Fantastic value!

I reported to the Canadian Agriculture Department in Toronto and was told to await their instructions. The harvest had not quite started. Prior to leaving the UK I had been introduced to a Canadian businessman who was staying with one of Father's friends (Ernie Dennis). This gentleman owned a supermarket on Young Street (Pickering Farms) in Toronto and he offered to give me a job if I needed one. I took up his offer and was given the job of restocking shelves in the supermarket. This was a lousy job which didn't suit me, and after two weeks I was looking for something else. I saw an ad in a Toronto magazine (Harpers, I think) which said 'See Canada' etc. I took time off and went for an interview. It turned out to be selling subscriptions. That wouldn't suit me either! I cut short the interview and left. When I returned to the supermarket I was fired, which did suit me!

When I was in Toronto the underground railway under Young Street was being constructed. This caused much disruption in Young Street, as there were numerous huge access points from the road above (not just potholes!)

Luckily, Mother had put me in touch with one of her farmer friends who had a son, Edwin, who was working in Canada. I gave him a call and asked if he knew of a farmer who needed some help. Edwin phoned me back in a couple of days. Next day I got a bus to Orangeville, about 50 miles north of Toronto, and began working for Carson Patterson on his mixed farm at Mona Mills. I stayed with Carson, his wife Mildred and young son Robert as part of the family, for the next two months or so. It was a very pleasant time. Carson's farm was mixed, with beef cattle, potatoes and corn. He used one Shire horse and a Farmall tractor. He was a good man to work for.

Some parts of Canada were 'dry', no alcohol – this was Prohibition. Those who couldn't go without had to drive about 40 miles to the nearest pub. I enjoyed a pint or two and one day I was taken the 40 miles to the 'local'. It was an interesting experience. Customers were not allowed to stand at the bar but had to sit at a table. A waiter bought the drinks, two at a time. Several clients ended up under the table. Once was enough for me.

On one free weekend I was joined by Edwin. He had a car and we took off and camped on the edge of Georgian Bay, where we hired a wooden boat with an outboard motor. Some distance from the shore we hit a large submerged log which put a hole in the boat. The boat quickly filled with water and we had to swim for the shore, pulling the boat with us. Lucky it was wooden. We managed to get it ashore but had to pay the owner a considerable amount of cash before he would let us go. He emptied our pockets!

When Carson had finished harvesting I contacted the Department of Agriculture (D of A) in Toronto and was told to travel by rail to Calgary, Alberta, and report to their office there. The harvest in the west is considerably later than in Ontario. The journey to Calgary took three days and I had a stopover for one night in the Windy City, Winnipeg, where I bought some winter clothes from the Hudson Bay Company Store. I stayed in the City YMCA youth hostel, which was like a hotel.

Before Winnipeg, which is in Manitoba, the train passed through Sudbury and Sault Ste Marie in Ontario. The countryside in this area is mainly forest and quite wild. Canada is a massive country!

Beyond Winnipeg, the train crossed Saskatchewan, where the prairies began, calling at Regina and Moose Jaw before entering Alberta near Medicine Hat. All these names had connections with Red Indians who before the British settlers arrived had occupied all this part of Canada. In 1951 when I was there the Indians mostly lived in reserves, although a small number were gradually integrating with the newcomers.

Once in Calgary, the D of A issued me with the name and contact details of the farmer I was to help. He was from the Ukraine and farmed about 1000 acres on the Alberta prairie. The nearest town and railhead was Red Deer. The famer met me at the station in his pickup truck and took me the 40 miles along pretty rough roads (no tarmac) to the farm, which was all arable, mostly wheat. All the harvesting was by men and horses. The soil was quite unlike soil in the UK. It was deep black and

The coyote (left photo), had a very eerie howl and the prairie dogs (groundhogs) (above) popped up all over the place

called 'gumbo'. Two Ukrainians farmed the land together and hired a gang for the harvest. I was one of the gang, which was made up of some odd characters. Several of them were Red Indians without their feathers. One was a Dutchman who I had met on the *Georgic* on the way out. The accommodation was in a 'bunkhouse' which slept about 10 men. Many hadn't washed for weeks and the stench was unbearable. Fortunately the farmer's son had a tent which I was able to use. I slept in it until the end of November, when the harvest was complete. Sometimes it began to snow before it was finished. Not this time!

A binder was used to cut the wheat and tie it into sheaves. The gang's first job was to 'Stook' the sheaves ready for them to be collected by horse and wagon. With a thousand acres to Stook, this was quite a task. Stooking had the effect of keeping the grain away from the damp ground and was convenient for loading on to the horse-drawn wagons.

A wagon and horses similar to ones I used. My final load was nearly twice as high!

When the stooking was complete I was allocated an almost new rubber-tyred wagon and a pair of Canadian Percherons. These belonged to a neighbouring farmer, Mr James. He also had the first John Deere combine in the area, but this was not used on the farm where I was working. The 'gang' reported for duty at six in the morning, fed and watered the horses and then had a real 'proper' breakfast. Each member of the gang was allocated a pair of horses. I was privileged, as my pair of Percherons were superb. They had been very well schooled. A whistle was the signal to walk on and another told them to stop. If we were working some distance from the farmstead, I rode one and led the other. All the others walked!

Each gang member had to load his wagon and drive it to the threshing machine, then unload it himself into the machine, which was driven by a British single-cylinder Field Marshal tractor. This tractor was started by exploding a cartridge! A very good tractor, but noisy. We worked until dusk. Getting the harvest in quickly was critical to avoid the possibility of snow. This year they were lucky and the crop was good. The corn was put in portable silos or, if they were full, in heaps on the ground, to be collected later when it would be taken by truck to the nearest Railhead, Red Deer, some 40 miles away.

One particular wagonload was quite eventful. I had loaded the wagon as high as I could manage, climbed aboard and set out for the thresher. Suddenly one of the Percherons went bananas. It had stepped on a porcupine, which shot its quills into his legs. I was only just able to prevent the pair from bolting. Fortunately one of the farmers spotted the problem and was soon on the scene with some rope. He detached the horses from the wagon, a central pole, got the rope around the affected horse's legs and gently pulled him to the ground. While I held this massive, beautiful 17-hand animal he extracted the needles with pliers, and we were soon on the move again.

When it came to the last load the whole gang helped me load my wagon and I was on top. There was no ladder and I had to jump from about 20 feet. No problem -always bend your knees!

When we completed the work on this farm we moved to another, which was some five miles away. This holding, farmed by an old

Englishman, was very run down and the crops were very poor. This time I used his pair of old Shires and a rough cart. On one load I climbed aboard and shook the rains to go. The horses took off with the front wheels and left me stranded with the rest!

When the harvest was finished I heard that a fairly close neighbour who had a cattle ranch needed some help. I moved to the ranch and did a bit of 'Cowboying'. It was a pretty rough outfit. Several other chaps working on local oil drilling rigs were accommodated in the farmhouse. One day a skunk appeared in the dining room. The smell was awful. I soon moved on.

The Banff Springs Hotel

I now had until the 15th of December to make the return journey to the UK to qualify for the £15 return fare. This would start from Calgary. I wanted to see as much of the west of Canada and the USA as possible in the two weeks I had left. I decided to hitch-hike to Vancouver if possible, and set out walking on the road towards Banff in the Canadian Rockies, some 85 miles away. Very quickly a car stopped and the driver was going to Banff. He was a Mr Watts, who originated from Torquay in Devon. He was in charge of the municipal gardens in Banff, which were quite outstanding.

Mr Watts advised that it would be impossible to travel through the Rockies by road at that time of year as the roads would be snowbound until the following spring, so I should proceed by rail. I stayed with the Watts family for a couple of nights and was shown around the area and

Not so far from the hotel I was taken to a large rubbish dump which was a favourite spot for brown bears. I kept my distance!

particularly the Banff Springs Hotel. I had a swim in the super outdoor pool, where the water came hot out of the ground like the Roman Baths in Bath.

I duly caught the overnight train which would take me to Vancouver. However, to conserve my hard-earned cash, I decided to leave the train once it had cleared the Rockies at Revelstoke and hitch-hike once more. I popped into a café for coffee and breakfast and sat next to a young English lad. He was a truck driver who happened to be driving back to Vancouver after his breakfast, and he offered me a lift. This was just what the doctor ordered, and within three or four hours I was in Vancouver. The route took me through Kamloops and then followed the Fraser River through some beautiful country. Vancouver is quite special and I particularly remember the Indian totem poles in one of the parks.

After a couple of days I boarded the ferry to Victoria, Vancouver Island. Victoria was quite quaint and was much like England would have been 100 years earlier. From there I took the Ferry to Seattle, which was not far away. To get there you go through the Puget Sound and on this particular passage the sound, and Seattle itself, were completely fogbound. I was happy to leave the fog behind and headed through Washington State, which, without the fog, is very beautiful. California here I come!

Hitch-hiking was forbidden in California, so I chose to take the Greyhound bus –they covered practically the entire USA. The journey took me through Tacoma in Washington and then Portland, Oregon and onwards through California to San Francisco. San Francisco is very special. It has an extremely steep hill from one end to the other which trams climb up and down. By the harbour is a large area known as Chinatown. In the harbour itself is the island of Alcatraz which, for many years, held the country's most dangerous prisoners. Very few ever escaped.

The prison island of Alcatraz in San Francisco Bay. Only one convict managed to escape. I think it was Clint Eastwood!

The Golden Gate Bridge spanning San Francisco Bay

To go south from San Francisco, you cross the Golden Gate Bridge to Berkley. I was heading for Los Angeles and on the way passed through Santa Barbara and then stopped off in Santa Monica. As I was gazing into a shop window a fellow of about 50 years old came up to me and we got into a conversation. He gathered that I was looking for somewhere to stay that night and offered to put me up in his flat. I accepted. It turned out that I would be sleeping in the same bed as him. This was not what I had in mind! I kept well to my side of the bed and survived the night untouched, but with little or no sleep! He was well meaning, fortunately.

I had a fairly quick look around Los Angeles and Hollywood. Neither appealed to me and I soon headed east by Greyhound to Las Vegas. The bus arrived there about 5 am on a very cold morning. Las Vegas, which is surrounded by desert, was nothing like it is today, though the beginnings of the gambling centre were apparent. I had a look around one gambling den. Not my scene, then or since!

Bearing in mind that I had to be back in Calgary by the 15th of December, I headed for Salt Lake City in Utah, which of course is the home of the religious sect the Mormons, who practise polygamy. Many have several wives. The city is quite beautiful, especially the Mormon cathedral. The route from Salt Lake City (there is a massive salt lake nearby where land speed records have been broken) to Calgary took me through Montana. No Greyhound buses on this route, but I found a bus which would take me most of the way. I was the only white man on the bus, as the rest were all Red Indians, or Native Americans as we call them now (the Blackfoots). Luckily they were friendly and kept themselves to themselves. We passed a few herds of buffalo.

In Calgary I signed off at the Department of Agriculture and was given my return rail ticket. Once I had this there was no rush, and I planned to go back to Carson Patterson before catching the boat home. Shortly after my arrival, father phoned from the UK. Among the farmers

A Blackfoot Indian. Many still live in reservations. Except on ceremonial occasions they now dress the same as other Americans.

A herd of buffalo (bison). Indians relied on the buffalo for their meat and skins, with which they made their wigwams and clothes. Very few remain.

who sold their eggs to Waldens was Geoffrey Sykes, a very progressive farmer who had recently been to the USA to study the poultry industry. Two or three others in the UK had also been there and were setting up packing stations to handle broiler chicken. Geoffrey Sykes knew that Waldens were handling hens and suggested that while I was the other side of the Atlantic I too should study the US poultry business. I was told to contact a Joe Sutton, who was a chick sexer in Mount Vernon, Illinois. I did what I was told and arranged to go to Mount Vernon and stay with Joe Sutton after the winter, which I spent with Carson and his family helping enough to pay for my keep.

Canadian winters are extremely cold. Carson had a good-size pond which was soon frozen solid. I was able to borrow some skates and had some great fun on the pond.

The winter went quite quickly and in the spring I set off for Mount Vernon. I managed to hitch from Buffalo (New York State), having crossed from Canada by Niagara Falls, to Detroit, which is, or was, famous as the HQ of the Ford empire. From there I got another lift to Chicago. I spent a few days in Chicago, which is well worth a visit. It is on Lake Michigan and has a super natural history museum, one of the best in the world. There are also some good theatres and I was able to see Ethel Merman in 'Call Me Madam' and Danny Kaye in 'Hans Christian Andersen'. Both were very good.

Another point of interest is that the railways in Chicago run overhead. This is very noisy, especially if you are staying close to them. I visited the very extensive cattle market, which had a section dealing with poultry. The first thing I learned was that at that time, practically all poultry in the USA was both transported and sold packed in ice.

After about a week I headed for Mount Vernon and managed to hitch there. I carried a Union Jack, and this helped. One particular car that stopped for me contained a load of drunks, so at the driver's first stop I made an excuse and got out. I soon found a lift with a sober driver. I found that by and large the Americans are very friendly and generous, even when not quite sober!

I had made contact with Joe Sutton before leaving Ontario, and Joe met me and took me to his modern home. I stayed with him and his family for two weeks, during which time I learned almost all there was to know about the US poultry business. Joe took me to see a poultry-processing plant where they were handling over 100,000 chickens per week, a hatchery and a farm which raised 25,000 broiler chickens every three months. In addition Joe showed me around all the local places of interest, including a visit to the local high school. Here I had to address the pupils, and I was treated like royalty as it was quite rare for them to have a visitor from the UK. Later Father invited Joe to stay with us in Trowbridge and we were pleased to make him welcome. My visit to Mount Vernon and my stay with Joe Sutton were well worthwhile.

From Mount Vernon I headed east for New York. Among other places the Greyhound buses took me through the state of Indiana to Cincinnati, in Ohio, and then through West Virginia to Washington DC. The difference in each state was quite marked, particularly West Virginia.

I spent a couple of days in Washington and made sure I saw all the places of interest. The Abraham Lincoln Memorial has had a lasting

Greyhound bus

impression on me – he was a great man. From Washington I again used the Greyhound buses, which provided a jolly good service. This trip took me to New York via Baltimore and Philadelphia.

In New York I had about two weeks before boarding the RMS *Queen Elizabeth* for the voyage home. Fortunately father had paid the fare, which at that time was about £60! I had sufficient spare cash left from my work in Canada and I made good use of this in New York, seeing two or three shows on Broadway. Apart from the fact that the Duke of Windsor was on board, the return Atlantic crossing was uneventful and very pleasant. When I disembarked in Southampton I had precisely one farthing left in my pocket. I had enjoyed my trip to North America!

The Lincoln Memorial in Washington DC

Statue of Liberty

RMS Queen Elizabeth arriving at Ocean Terminal, Southampton, 1951/1952. The QE2 was perhaps the finest Cunard ship to sail the oceans. JW was fortunate to enjoy a voyage on this super ship in 2008 to the Mediterranean.

CHAPTER 8

JOINING THE FAMILY FIRM, 1952-1961

It was great to be home again, but I did not regret a moment of my time in North America. All youngsters should grasp whatever opportunity presents itself to travel and work for someone other than their parents before they get tied down with responsibilities.

Shortly before I had left home in 1951, my parents had moved to a much nicer property, Halfway Cottage on Hilperton Road, Trowbridge. It included 10 acres of pasture and some stabling (see my Chapter 15; "In the Saddle", on Horses and Hunting).

I had left a lovely Labrador bitch, Dinah, behind when I went to Canada. She had been very close to me, but when I returned she wouldn't have anything to do with me, which was quite upsetting. I guess I had let her down.

In about 1946, a year after WW2 had ended, father had bought a 40-acre holding at Ladydown, Trowbridge. Originally it was a pig farm, using swill to feed the pigs. The stench was unbearable and Henry soon dispensed with the pigs and the pigman. German POWs were used to re-fence the property. This property was less than a mile from the factory on the Down, which was rapidly being outgrown.

Just before my stint in Canada, Waldens had begun buying hens from local farmers, birds which had completed their laying lives. A large garage was built on the land at Ladydown for servicing and repairing the expanding fleet of sales vans. The hens were dealt with in part of that building using a dry plucking machine. As I had studied the American poultry industry, I was now, at the age of 22, given the job of developing this side of the business.

The main person employed on this project was an Italian ex-POW, Carlo Gondolfi. I worked with Carlo, who was a super fellow. Like a good many ex-prisoners of war he married a local girl and settled in Trowbridge. He and I worked together for several years, and soon we were joined by Harry Fielding, who had previously been a van salesman for the firm, and my cousin Donald Walden FCA, both of whom had returned from the war.

Quite soon a purpose-built factory was erected to handle the poultry business, which expanded steadily. The broiler chicken business was just beginning in the UK and Waldens were among the first six firms who pioneered this business. It is thanks to our joint efforts that chicken is now a major part of the British diet. In addition to dealing with the broiler chickens, hens and other poultry were processed, including large numbers of turkeys and capons for Christmas. In the USA all poultry were transported in ice, but at this time in the UK, refrigeration was at an early stage of development. It was widely used on ships to bring lamb and butter from New Zealand and beef from the Argentine, where the Vestey family of Dewhurst Butchers fame, had extensive farming interests. Union International, also part of the Vestey empire, imported frozen fish from South Africa in Union Castle ships. No mechanical refrigeration was available for road transport. To get our Christmas poultry orders to South Wales we initially used British Rail, which was a nationalized outfit. One consignment destined for the Ynysybwl Co-op among others in South Wales failed to arrive for Christmas. Later it was discovered in Worcester. So much for British Rail!

Throughout this period Harry Fielding was my right-hand man. At Christmas we sometimes had to work nearly all night to ensure that the Christmas orders were delivered on time. I owe Harry a great debt of thanks. He was a great guy.

Initially the birds, all sorts, were plucked with a Combe plucking machine, which was a dry and dusty process. To be effective it had to be done as soon as the bird was dead and still warm.

We gradually introduced wet plucking, then in its infancy. A large hot water tank was installed and the birds were dipped in this before being plucked by a machine which had fast-revolving rubber fingers. To begin with, this was all carried out by hand and was a very messy business. As soon as possible, when funds were available, an overhead

Poultry being plucked using Combe plucking machines, circa 1953. Later wet plucking was introduced, together with overhead conveyors. By about 1960 the plant was handling about 40,000 chicken per week. All the poultry were oven-ready and frozen. On the left is Dennis Pearce and the person pushing a rack of birds into the chill room is most likely Harry Fielding, my right-hand man! (See Chapter 1, Harry is in the photo of the firm's outing in 1936)

conveyor was installed, and this enabled us to handle quite large numbers each day.

Among my suppliers of hens, turkeys and capons were John Tarrant, John Carter and David Hitchings, all ex Dauntsey's School. Others were Ralph Carey of Potterne, Charles Davies of Bromham, the Walker brothers, Michael and Roy, of Chitterne, W R (Bill) Curnick of Burbage, Fred Snook of Urchfont, Raymond Rudler of Horton (both near Devizes), Geoffrey Sykes of Berwick St James, near Salisbury, Madge Hutton of Chippenham and Billy Gale of Warminster. The quality of their poultry, and that of many others, was first class and definitely contributed to the success of the business. Messer's Snook and Rudler were very large and successful farmers in the Pewsey Vale. Because they both drove Bentleys, the Vale was known as the "Bentley Vale". Fred's son, John, is still the proud owner of Fred's last classic Bentley, which is now extremely valuable.

For those who are interested, the technical definition of a capon is a chicken that has either been castrated or injected with a pill. Caponizing increases the rate of growth, plumptiousness and succulence! It is rarely used today and chicken are generally produced in vast numbers in order to keep the increasing population well fed.

An early "sporty" Bentley similar to the one owned by Fred Snook and his son John

Sainsbury's in London ordered 5 tons of eviscerated hens, which I took to London in a non-refrigerated van. When I got there, the Buyer, a Mr Justice, inspected them. Some were beginning to turn green. He refused to accept them and I returned to Trowbridge, where the whole load had to be destroyed. Quite a setback! No more business with

JW and J C J Tarrant, aged 80 and still good friends! (2012)

Sainsbury's. Luckily a Mr Chippendale-Higgin (a descendant of the renowned furniture maker) had approached me offering to sell our poultry in London, particularly to H J Heinz. I met Mr C-H in London and together we went to the Heinz factory. We were shown around by the Buyer, a Mr Lewin, and then discussed business. Heinz needed large quantities of hen meat for their chicken soup. Fortunately, following the Sainsbury fiasco, we had recently installed a large freezing plant, supplied by J and E Hall of Dartford in Kent. The Heinz order was exactly what was needed. It was for 100 tonnes of hen meat and 20 tonnes of hen fat.

Further orders followed once the first one was completed. The price paid by Heinz was exceptionally good and it enabled me to pay the farmers the best price available for their hens.

There was another gent in London who contacted me at about this time to offer his services to sell our poultry. His name was Livingstone-Learmouth (LL). I met him in London and he took me to Ronnie Scott's Jazz Club. Who should be in the club but the famous film star Kenneth More. It was slightly embarrassing, as we met in the gents. I didn't ask him for his autograph! LL didn't sell any poultry, but I enjoyed Ronnie Scott's!

At this stage, the only method of keep the poultry frozen in transit was to use blocks of 'cardice', solid CO_2 supplied by ICI. The next stage was the use of large bottles of CO2. These were strapped inside the van body and the gas released gradually during the journey. Both of the above would hold a fairly low temperature for about 12 hours in a well-insulated vehicle. On one occasion one of these massive bottles broke loose in transit and crashed out through the rear doors on to the road. Fortunately no damage or harm was done to other road users.

In time, Petters of Southampton produced a mechanical unit which we used, and these and other makes from the USA (Thermal King) and France were soon in regular use. Alan and Barry Noakes built a number of our insulated van bodies at their workshop at Ladydown. Archie Bennett, a skilled pattern maker, Bill Thicket and Ted Tandy were all employed by Waldens to make anything in timber.

Collecting the poultry was also an area which needed developing. Initially we used an ancient Ford truck which was much like a truck version of a Ford Model T car. Soon we added a Land Rover and a rice trailer which was made especially for the job. We used Gages, each containing about 50 hens, and the trailer carried four of these, which were on castors. As the volume increased, so did the size of the trucks we used. There was a 5-tonne Bedford and later a 7-tonne American Dodge, which would carry over a thousand chickens in wooden crates. Early one morning a full load which was on its way to the packing plant from the Chippenham area turned over on its side, dumping the loaded crates of chicken over a hedge and onto the road. I was called to help deal with the problem. It was complete chaos for quite a while. No one was hurt and 80% of the chickens reached the factory, though much later than planned! Later I introduced demountable flatbeds (called Cargons) which were wheeled on and off the trucks on to a loading bay.

Some years later, after my time in the poultry Industry, articulated trucks with 40 foot trailers were introduced which would carry 2000 chickens or more per load.

Gradually, I persuaded local farmers to erect broiler chicken houses which each housed 5,000, 10,000 or 20,000 birds. My father, with my youngest brother Ben, erected a 5000-bird unit at Halfway Cottage for demonstration purposes, and this was a great help. The objective was to provide a steady flow of plump chickens to keep the factory and its employees busy on a regular basis. In addition the customers, which included Lewis' stores in Liverpool, Manchester, Birmingham and Bristol, David Grieg's many Branches, Walter Smith, butchers in Birmingham with about twenty shops, and a considerable number of Co-ops in South Wales all of which had to be guaranteed a regular supply.

At this stage I was doing the buying and the selling. Soon I employed a couple of salesmen, one in Birmingham and one in Cardiff. Jim Smith, in Cardiff, had a well-established connection with the South Wales Co-ops and his orders for Christmas poultry were substantial.

Many American service personnel were still based in the UK, and I was approached by them to see if we could supply frozen portions of chicken specially packed in printed cartons, which we had to supply. We took the job on. We had only just begun to eviscerate chicken and the preparation of portions was entirely new. For each consignment an American vet had to be present, Lt Kelly. The main value from this venture was that we quickly learnt how to go about the job and Lt Kelly was very helpful. Part of the learning curve!

As the volume increased more overhead conveyors were installed and many additional staff engaged. One of them came from Hungary – he had recently left his homeland to escape the Russians. Unfortunately he had light fingers. Another member of staff reported that money had been stolen from her coat, which had been hung up in a cloakroom. I called the local constabulary and a trap was set. A number of £1 and £5 notes were dipped in a powder which would be visible when placed under a very bright lamp. The notes were put in the same person's pocket and, very quickly, these notes went missing too. The thief was caught red-handed and fired on the spot.

At that time there was no bridge across the River Severn. I made a number of trips to South Wales and had to use the Aust Ferry, which ceased to run at 9 pm. I missed it once and had to divert an extra 60 miles via Gloucester. Driving on an off the ferry in inclement weather was an adventure in itself, up and down a slippery ramp. On one trip to Wales, Jim introduced me to a number of his customers, the Co-op buyers. In Aberdare we had lunch in the Boot with the branch butchery manager. The food was good and so was the beer. It was a good thing that Jim was the driver!

Coinciding with my return from Canada my first cousin, Donald Withers Walden FCA, joined Waldens and became the Company Accountant. Donald had been in the Army in North Africa during the war. Initially, to begin with, Donald and I shared a quite small wooden hut as our office. Donald was a very special person, similar to Harry Fielding and Carlo Gondolfi, and was a great help to me. Donald made sure that I got my costings right. He and I worked together for 35 years during which time we never had a cross word. Having Donald to support me was a stroke of luck.

Other senior managers at Waldens who had served in WW2 were Ronald Courtier, the manager of the butter factory, Geoffrey Norris,

The Aust Ferry crossing to South Wales, first Severn Bridge under construction in the background, 1964

the Company Secretary, and Gordon Reed, Office Manager for the Bakery Department. Others who returned after the war were van sales men, including Ray Ward, Paul Stumbles and Roy Jones, all good chaps. Another stalwart was Betty Smith in the office.

William Donald Withers (Donald) Walden FCA. Accountant 1st Class!

It took a considerable time to make the Poultry Department a profitable unit. Eventually, with considerable effort, it started to make money and, in about 1961, a firm called Stirling Poultry, which owned a hatchery near Andover, approached Henry with an offer to buy this part of the Walden empire. By this time we were processing about 40,000 chickens per week and the factory was well mechanized using a continuous overhead conveyor system. The offer was good and Father encouraged and persuaded me to accept the sale.

To begin with I worked for the new owners, and within a short period the business was resold to the Ross Group, big trawler owners from Grimsby. They were keen to diversify from the fishing industry, which was shrinking, and move into poultry, which was rapidly expanding. Ross bought several poultry packing stations similar to Waldens. I worked for them for six months, during which time I had six managing directors! The final one from Boston, Lincolnshire, Bill

Newington (he had owned the Boston Mill chicken brand) made sure he learnt as much as possible from me and then told me to meet him in Bedford, where he gave me the sack! The Ross Group, in my opinion, was a ruthless outfit, quite different to Waldens. I was pleased to leave them and get six months' salary.

I had had enough of the poultry industry by this time. I took a short break, which gave me time to reflect and plan what I should do in the future. The frozen food industry was developing quite rapidly, and I was already well aware of its potential.

CHAPTER 9

HOMES AND PROPERTY, 1956-1971

Mead Cottage to Knights Marsh Farm
via Barn Cottage, Great Hinton

In 1956 at the age of 25 I married Ann Meakin, who lived at Minety in North Wiltshire. Ann had trained as a nurse at St Thomas's Hospital in London and was also a qualified midwife. Ann's father, Colin, was a lovely man and quite a character. His family were part of the famous pottery family, J and G Meakin, from Stoke-on-Trent, in Staffordshire. Colin was, possibly, the black sheep of the family. He spent much of his early life in Canada and the USA where, amongst other interesting activities, like gold prospecting, he was in the North-West Mounted Police.

Colin's obituary which appeared in the *Wiltshire Gazette* is quite interesting:

Colin, age 19, went to Canada. Tiring of farm work he joined company with Sioux Indians and hunted deer and moose in the River Mountains. When the season was over, he teamed up with Pat Burns Riders as a cow puncher. He grew tired of life on the range and joined the North-West Mounted Police. About three years later he moved south to Costa Rica and worked on a large banana plantation. He resumed his travels and ventured to Australia and worked on sheep farms. After a lucky gold strike he returned to Minety in 1928 to settle down. He married Dorothy Ponting. Before doing so he joined the British Army and served with distinction throughout WW1. As you can imagine he had many stories to tell of which his children loved to hear. Ann (married John Walden), John (John's best friend at school) and Dick.

Having recently (October 2014) had a very pleasant stay with Colin's son John and his wife Elizabeth, now retired and living in Tavistock, Devon, I cleaned some more details of Colin's adventures. As an adventurous young man, Colin, having returned from his travels, as briefly described above, returned to the UK at the outset of World War 1, joined the army. Initially he went to Sandhurst to be trained as an officer. Like many young men he and his colleagues were quite boisterous and frequently got up to mischief in their off-duty hours. On one occasion, Colin, with some friends, had rather an excessive amount of beer. In their somewhat intoxicated condition, they decided to push a cannon weighing nearly two tons into a stream which bordered Sandhurst. With considerable effort and obviously with great hilarity they succeeded. Colin, along with most of those involved, was immediately discharged from Sandhurst. Being very patriotic, he then joined a Calvary Regiment. Very soon he was sent to France and thence to the front line, which was, at that time, being decimated by the superior German army. It was quickly established that cavalry regiments were no line of defence, were completely outdated and unfit for purpose. Many hundreds of horses were slaughtered early in the war and very few survived to return to the UK.

Colin spent the next three years or so in the trenches which, as is widely known, were horrific. Colin didn't tell his children, John, Ann (my first wife) and Richard much about this part of his life. One thing which did come to light is that on one occasion, in a trench, he was standing by a colleague when a shell missed him by about a foot. He turned to find that his colleague's head had been completely blown off.

Colin was a very lucky man; unlike many tens of thousands of others, he came home at the end of the war sound in wind and limb. I have no doubt that it would have taken a long time for Colin to adjust to normal life after his return. He produced three fine children.

Colin and Dorothy Meakin. Circa: 1927.

I had saved some money towards buying my first house, Mead Cottage, Victoria Road, Trowbridge, but not enough. The price was £5000. Father loaned me a £1000 towards it and with some help from the Midland Bank I was able to complete the purchase. About a year later I honoured my agreement with father and repaid the £1000.

Mead Cottage was a very modern house with a large walled garden. It had been part of Rodwell Hall which originally belonged to one of the local cloth mill owners. At this time, Rodwell Hall was split in two.

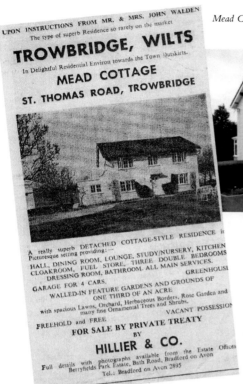

Mead Cottage, 1962 advertisement

UPON INSTRUCTIONS FROM MR. & MRS. JOHN WALDEN
The type of superb Residence so rarely on the market

TROWBRIDGE, WILTS

In Delightful Residential Environ towards the Town Outskirts.

MEAD COTTAGE
ST. THOMAS ROAD, TROWBRIDGE

A really superb DETACHED COTTAGE-STYLE RESIDENCE in Picturesque setting providing:—
HALL, DINING ROOM, LOUNGE, STUDY/NURSERY, KITCHEN CLOAKROOM, FUEL STORE, THREE DOUBLE BEDROOMS DRESSING ROOM, BATHROOM. ALL MAIN SERVICES.
GREENHOUSE
GARAGE FOR 4 CARS.
WALLED-IN FEATURE GARDENS AND GROUNDS OF
ONE THIRD OF AN ACRE
with spacious Lawns, Orchard, Herbaceous Borders, Rose Garden and many fine Ornamental Trees and Shrubs.
VACANT POSSESSION
FREEHOLD and FREE
FOR SALE BY PRIVATE TREATY
BY

HILLIER & CO.

Full details with photographs available from the Estate Offices
Berryfields Park Estate, Bath Road, Bradford on Avon
Tel.: Bradford on Avon 2895

Mead Cottage, St Thomas's Road, Trowbridge 2014. The right hand part is the original when occupied by JW in 1958.

One part was occupied by my doctor, Rodney Pearce and the other by my Solicitor, Tony King. Both became friends and we often played squash together in a squash court in Devizes Market Place. Tony was an outstanding squash player, far better than Rodney or me. Later I taught Tony to sail.

Mead Cottage didn't really suit me as I preferred to live in the country. Our three children were born there. Unfortunately Jane, the firstborn, was ill from birth and never walked. She was sick continually from day one and the doctors thought the trouble was a hiatus hernia (blockage of the digestive system causing continuous sickness). She spent the first two years of her life sat in a specially made chair. In spite of this she was very bright. She was a chatterbox and quickly learnt all the nursery rhymes. But at two years old it was noticed that Jane's head was becoming enlarged. Jane was taken to Frenchay Hospital in Bristol, where they opened up her skull. The findings were terrible. The whole brain was entwined in a cancerous growth and was inoperable. Poor Jane, she deteriorated very quickly and passed away when she was only 2½ years old. She was buried in Hilperton Cemetery, near Trowbridge. It was a sad time as Jane was a very special, happy little girl. Later Hugh John was born and then Sarah Jane who were, and are, two good robust individuals.

JW's wedding, with brothers Ben, on left, and Michael on right

JW's wedding day

Jane's grave at Hilperton, 1960

Hugh, John, Ann and Sarah Walden at Mead cottage, 1960

At this time Waldens' poultry business was developing quite rapidly and Victoria Road was the main route for vehicles "toing and froing" from the Factory at Ladydown. As I was involved with the transport it regularly disturbed my beauty sleep, so much so that after five years I was ready to move on (that was my excuse!) One weekend I visited my cousin, Neville Giddings, who was farming at Watts Farm, Great Hinton. (Neville was originally from Manor Farm Sandridge, Melksham). Both our families were having tea in his garden when a neighbour, a Mr Stocken, popped his head over the hedge for a chat during which he said "Would you like to buy my property?" He described the property, which had six acres of ground, and said he wanted £10,000 for it. I indicated that I was very interested but would have to sell Mead Cottage before I could commit myself.

I quickly put Mead Cottage on the market at £10,000 and found a buyer within a couple of weeks. We moved to Great Hinton in about 1961. The property was called Barn Cottage and needed a lot of work to get it to a reasonable standard. It had a barn and a building which could be used as a stable. On three of the acres, Mr Stocken had been

Barn Cottage, Great Hinton. Note strawberry cloches on left.

growing strawberries. My wife, Ann, had green fingers. Mr Stocken taught us how to grow strawberries and we grew them successfully for the next eight or so years. Many were sold to Don Ship, who had a very good greengrocery shop in Silver Street, Trowbridge. In WW2 Don had been General Montgomery's driver in his Humber staff car. Now that I had some land, it wasn't long before I bought my first horse, Raspella.

The Great Hinton property had valid planning permission on three acres of the land. As this would eventually expire if it was not used, we decided to see if we could find somewhere else to live which would be more suitable for horses and in better riding country. One weekend Father and I boxed up two horses from his home in Trowbridge and headed for Roundway Down just above Devizes and hacked over the downs to Heddington, near Calne. In Heddington we popped into the Ivy Inn, where William Pitt was the popular landlord. After a pint of Wadsworth's 6X and a sandwich, we rode back to Devizes. Over the next 25 years or so, Father and I often rode out together and this was one of the highlights of my life. This particular outing convinced me that the Heddington area would be a good place to live

Shortly after the visit to the Ivy in Heddington, Ann was scanning the Wiltshire Gazette and spotted an ad which said that Knights Marsh Farm in Stockley Lane, Calne was soon to be sold by auction. We contacted the owner, Harold Marsh, and were shown round the farm. The property needed quite a lot done to it to bring it up to modern standards, but that did not put us off. We decided that if we could raise the money we would bid at the auction, which was the following week.

I approached my then Midland Bank manager, Jimmy Macmillan, a nephew of Harold Macmillan, one time Prime Minister, requesting a bridging loan. I had established that Barn Cottage would be worth about 35K taking into account the value of the building land. Jimmy turned down my request. Ann was banking next door at Lloyds. I made an appointment to see the manager and he said "How much do you want"? I named my figure and went to the auction knowing that I could bid up to a maximum figure of about £36,000 for the 70-acre property.

I took one of Sylvester and Macketts' solicitors, Peter Robjant, to the auction to make sure I didn't "step over the mark". It was quite exciting and the price I paid for the 75-acre farm was 25K. Steps were taken to sell Barn Cottage. A buyer (or two) was found and the property was quickly sold for 36K.

Harold Marsh and his son Michael were dairy farmers and were milking a herd of some 40 Friesian cattle at Knights Marsh Farm. The milking parlour was attached to the farmhouse and the water tanks for cooling the milk etc. were installed in an upstairs room in the house above the kitchen. Close by, at the rear of the house were wooden cow kennels. The trend in farming, at this time, was that small dairy units were becoming uneconomical and were being swallowed up by larger units. It was not my intention to go into dairying, so I took steps to sell the cow kennels and remove the milking parlour.

The farmhouse was in a pretty bad shape. I understand from Wiltshire County Council Archives in County Hall Trowbridge that Knights Marsh Farm had been occupied since around the 11th Century , the first occupant being John Le Knight. It had been rebuilt and added to several times and the south-eastern section was obviously a fairly recent add-on, possibly a hundred years or so. This section had a slate tile roof which was in good shape. It had the main heavy front door which was so draughty that we sealed it up! The south-facing older section (some 400 years old or more) had a stone roof which was in very bad shape. On the ground floor there were two doors, one at the front and one at the back with rooms either side of a passage, one being the kitchen and the other a dining/living room. There were stairs from the kitchen to the room above where the dairy water tanks were. Additionally there were stairs in the other section from the entrance hall and the main front door. At the rear of the house was an area covered by a galvanized tin roof which contained the bathroom, WC and utilities.

As the house needed a major rebuild I contacted the Building Surveyor at North Wilts District Council a) to get his advice and b) to establish whether I could obtain a grant to make the necessary and essential improvements. The response was extremely helpful and positive. I got help and a grant!

A good builder was introduced to me, Michael Pitman, and it was agreed that he would carry out the work. This included a new tiled roof. When the old one was removed it exposed massive oak beams, both in the roof structure and in the ceilings. I was advised by an expert that they would have come out of Henry VIII's warships. Several were rotten and were replaced with some from the sawmills at Broughton Gifford, near Melksham. The best ones were re-used. The passage walls were demolished and the two rooms turned into one. This made a good living cum dining room with a modern kitchen, including an Aga which my father gave me. The cost at that time was about £350. Today it would be £5000 or more. This was in 1971. Forty years later it is still cooking and heating the water! The surplus front door in this part of the house was replaced by a window. The floors throughout the house were flagstones and these were all replaced by concrete. The concrete one in the kitchen/dining area I covered with quarry tiles over ½" of insulation. The dining area was carpeted over the tiles. Jack and Michael Cuthbert, the local electrical company, rewired the whole property. A new bathroom, WC and shower were installed upstairs and the outside lean-to was rebuilt to provide a utility area and an office. Initially this had a flat felt roof. After about 30 years this rotted and was replaced by tiles which were fitted by my neighbour at that time, Tony Burgess.

Bearing in mind the limited funds available, this was a great improvement and made a very comfortable home. How Knights Marsh Farm developed is described in Chapter 14.

Ann with Bonny at Stockley Hunter Trials, held at Knights Marsh Farm

Just word about property ownership: If it is possible for any individual, or couple, to save enough to buy their first home, then go for it as early in life as your can. Avoid renting - there is nothing like owning your own home. "An Englishman's home is his castle!" Maggie Thatcher was absolutely right when, as Prime Minister in 1980, she passed a Bill in Parliament to give tenants of council houses the right to buy. Good on you Maggie! It was noticeable in Trowbridge that within a short time, the houses on the Seymour Estate which had become privately owned were all spruced up, gardens blossoming, lawns and hedges cut, whereas the ones rented were looking decidedly tardy and unloved.

It was with very considerable regret that Ann and I separated in about 1976 and were divorced. I'm afraid that in the end we weren't compatible. I bought Ann a very pleasant cottage in Heddington, Fair View, and we remained good friends.

Fairview, Heddington. Joined to it on the left and part of the property is a very quaint cottage similar to the one in the nursery rhyme "Old Mother Hubbard"

Fairview in 2014. The left hand cottage has been modernised and extended.

Knights Marsh Farmhouse after it had been restored.

Ann remarried, but I remained single for the next seven years, which I did not enjoy. Luckily I had my good horses and my business life was successful. Sadly Ann passed away in 2006.

In 1983 I was recommended by a Polish person working for Waldens to contact a woman doctor in Warsaw, Poland who was single and looking for an English husband. I made contact by letter and phone (no

JW on right with his grandson, Daniel Boothe, Sarah's son, by Ann's grave at Heddington Cemetery, 2013

email then) and decided that I liked her. I went to Warsaw and on the second visit we were married. Her name was Barbara and she was a paediatrician practising in the main children's hospital in Warsaw.

Barbara came to Knights Marsh Farm in 1984 and we had two fine sons, Sam and Joseph Henry. I'm afraid that marrying a person from a foreign country, which at that time was still under communism, has its problems. Not only are our cultures very different, but Barbara was a city girl, whereas I was and still am very much a countryman. Not only are there the differences mentioned above, but there is also the problem for any newcomer arriving in the UK, and that is homesickness. This, in Barbara's case, became a quite serious problem. In addition to the cultural differences, I was prevented from keeping horses and, worse still, discouraged from contacting my family and many friends, mostly in the farming fraternity. I guess I had made a serious mistake! I did, however, enjoy bringing up our two boys, Sam and Joseph, and the family camping holidays we had. Not all bad news!

Fortunately, I was able to occupy myself in developing a new international campsite (See Chapter 12) (www.blacklandlakes.co.uk)

from scratch. Gradually, as the boys grew up, Barbara was determined to take over the business side of running the campsite, to the extent that I was sidelined. My business activity was put on hold for quite a long time, which was regrettable.

In 2005 a heart murmur which I had had for about 25 years became much worse. It proved to be a badly leaking mitral valve. It became apparent when I was sailing from Poole to the Solent with an inexperienced crew and I was forced to do a lot of the heavy work, such as pulling up the mainsail etc. I saw a cardiologist and then a surgeon at Bristol Royal Infirmary (BRI) and it was agreed that I should have an

Sam, Joseph and their mother Barbara, at Joseph's Graduation (BSc Automotive Engineering Oxford Brookes).

JW and Joseph, 2011

operation to repair the leaking valve. Before having the operation I went on a cruise to Holland with Sam and Joseph, in Sparky and Martin Pound in Lucy. I was glad I had two fit and capable lads with me and we had a super holiday. (See Chapter 15, Camping, Sailing etc.)

The next three years were the most unpleasant of my otherwise successful and happy life. It took two more open heart operations to sort out the problem. I now have a titanium valve. The first op in the Bristol Royal Infirmary, repaired the faulty valve, but ended up with me contracting MRSA which attacked and ruined the repair. The cleanliness, at that time, in the BRI left a lot to be desired. A year after I was given a titanium valve which

I had done privately in a much cleaner private clinic, The Glen, in Bristol. Unfortunately there was still a slight leak alongside the valve after this op, which caused me to pass out without warning. It took a three-month spell in the Queen Alexandra Hospital in Portsmouth before the cardiologist established the cause of my problem. I was sent to Southampton General Hospital for the third op and after a period of recuperation I have enjoyed very good health ever since.

Apart from regaining my health, the best thing worthy of mention is that apart from one failure at the Royal United Hospital in Bath and the poor standard of cleanliness at the BRI, I was very well looked after by all the National Health Service staff. I owe my life to them. Thank you, all of you!

Unfortunately my welcome on my return to Knights Marsh Farm after the first operation was quite negative. The developments over the next three years were quite unpleasant, to say the least. The situation became untenable and one morning in March 2007 I packed a bag and left. What followed is another story to be told at a later date. When considering this downturn in my otherwise good life I looked up the Magna Carta. In some ways it has a bearing on how things have developed for me during the period 2006 t0 2014. It is still a valid document, even in the 21st Century, and I quote it below:

Magna Carta
(Issued by King John at Runneymede near Windsor in 1215 and confirmed in British Law in 1297)

No Freeman shall be taken or imprisoned, or disseised of his freehold, or liberties, or free Customs or be outlawed or otherwise destroyed, nor we pass upon him or condemn him, but by lawful Judgement of his Peers, or by the Law of the Land; we seek to no man, we will not deny to any man either justice or right.

Due to the shortcomings and flaws in the present legal system, serious illness and the actions of various individuals, I have been deprived of my property, Knights Marsh Farm, and the business, Blackland Leisure Ltd, since 2007. In 2014, I am pleased to say that I am enjoying life and good health, although the legal problems have yet to be resolved.

CHAPTER 10

REDUNDANCY AND RECOVERY, 1961–2006

Waldens Wiltshire Foods Ltd

So in 1961 I found myself redundant, which was quite a shock. From the experience I had had with the Ross Group my opinion of them was not particularly high. They were not the best example of the capitalist system, which in the right hands, is better than any other. I suspect that the very tough conditions involved in running a fleet of deep sea trawlers had greatly influenced their view on business, which would have been quite different to mine or my family.

The original Waldens business centred on The Down was beginning to feel the effects of the increasing dominance of supermarkets. The smaller shops were unable to compete and were closing almost daily. Many of these had been Waldens customers since the firm started with butter in 1926. Even if I was interested, there was not an opening for me there. I had to make a fresh start. A new door had to be opened, and I was ready for the challenge.

Apart from the original factory on The Down, Waldens, having sold the poultry packing business and a large area of land with it, retained about 12 acres at Ladydown at the bottom of Canal Road, and this is where we now developed. Earlier, a greater part of the original 40 acres had been sold to Airsprung, who were making vast quantities of beds and other furniture. Ladydown, which is now the Canal Road Industrial Estate, was rapidly becoming the major industrial area in Trowbridge. Much of this can be attributed to the Walden family and to my father in particular.

A parcel of land at the top of the 12 acres had been sold to David Grieg, who used it as their distribution depot for several years. Grieg's, who were based in London, had many shops which previously had been one of my best customers for Farmer Jim chicken. Unlike Sainsbury's, who at that time had similar shops to David Grieg and opened up supermarkets, David Grieg chose not to and actually closed the business down. In my view this was quite sad, as they had a very good business with over 30 shops.

Waldens bought Grieg's depot back and opened it up as our first supermarket. This began as a cash and carry. The egg packing business, which wasn't included in the sale to Ross, was passed to Henry's younger brother Leslie. It is now run, successfully, by his two sons Robert and Tim and grandson Nicholas, who trade as Ashton Farms.

Michael transferred his responsibilities from egg packing to developing the supermarket business. In the course of time, Waldens were successfully operating four supermarkets. Four of Michael's right-hand personnel were Charles and Lilian Davies, Margaret Jones in the office, and David Perry, his first store manager. Charles Davies previously farmed in Bromham and in earlier days I purchased his super turkeys and nice fat hens.

Michael and David Perry outside the first supermarket at Ladydown

My father Henry on the occasion of Charles and Lilian Davies' retirement in 1981 from Waldens' Supermarket in Canal Road, Trowbridge. Henry passed away in 1983.

Waldens now began to develop the remaining 10 acres of developable land at Ladydown. the frozen food market was now progressing steadily and Henry and I decided that this was where the future lay, although we had no idea how it would develop.

We agreed to build a cold store, initially with the distribution of frozen food in mind. The required refrigeration unit was purchased from Prestcold of Oxford, who also advised on the design of the cold store. While this was being built I had to decide what products I should sell and from whom I would obtain them. As I was very familiar with the poultry business I approached Buxted Chicken, who previously had been my major competitor. Buxted agreed to supply me with their poultry and this was a major step in the right direction. Very quickly I was able to offer a good range of frozen food. Two refrigerated vans were bought and van salesmen engaged. I was in business once again!

My main customers were caterers, mostly pubs, many of whom were now offering cooked food. My first Cold Store Manager was Colin White (Colin is in the picture taken at the long service celebration of

An early photo of some of the Walden family, plus Joan and Gordon Reed. On the left: Joan Reed, Gordon Reed, Brenda and Donald Walden. On the right: Ben Walden, Jenny Walden, Phyllis Walden and John Walden. Photo taken on a company outing by rail to Paignton in Devon, 1960

A family and company group photo. From left: Ann Walden, John Walden, Margaret Daly (meal production) Gillian Walden, Michael Walden, Henry Walden, Donald Walden, Phyllis Walden, Brenda Walden, Phillip Yates (Phillip managed the frozen pie factory), Shelagh Molloy, (Sales Office). 1970

The 'Three Musketeers', JW, Ben and Michael, in harmony, 1965

Colin, Dennis Gerrish, Ray Ward and two ladies later in this chapter). He used to cycle to and from Keevil daily, some five miles from Trowbridge, come rain or shine. Colin was a super fellow who had previously served in the Royal Navy. He was on the Battleship HMS *Duke of York*, which brought the then Princess Elizabeth and Prince Phillip back from their holiday in South Africa following the death of King George VI. (Since writing this I have established that the Prince and Princess were flown back by a famous early aviator who was the boss of the forerunner of British Airways. His name escapes me.)

As time went on Waldens became well established in the frozen food trade. As I had had considerable experience in the distribution of frozen poultry I considered the possibility of carrying other companies' frozen products. With this in mind I investigated the question of obtaining a road haulage licence to do so. This was easier said than done! I was successful, after quite a struggle (see Chapter 11).

In about 1965 I received a phone call from a John Rolls, a main agent for Barbeque King Rotary Ovens. John (JR) was based in Bristol and covered the southern counties for the importers, who were based in Reading. These American-built ovens were designed to be used in shops for the in-store baking of pies, pasties and sausage rolls etc. JR was looking for a supplier of frozen pies. He came to see me, and once I had discussed the possibilities with Henry and my youngest brother Ben, who had recently joined the firm, it was decided that it would be a great opportunity to switch from fresh to frozen pies, and this is what we did. It proved to be an important milestone for the Walden business.

As quickly as possible a new factory was built at Ladydown and appropriate chilled, cold storage and freezing plant were installed. As soon as the new building was ready the pie section in the factory on the Down was moved to Ladydown. JR put us in touch with his customers and the frozen pie business was born. Barbeque King had other agents who they put in touch with me, especially one in Newark, Nottinghamshire.

While this was developing, the Transport Section had become well established. As customers for the frozen pies were found, the refrigerated vehicles were able to deliver them wherever they were required. The transport business was called Frigfreight (pronounced Fridgefreight, see

Waldens' site at Ladydown, Trowbridge, frozen food production units on the right and No 2 Cold Store on the left. The red brick building in the distance is Ladydown Mill. The railway line runs between. Late 1960s.

Any excuse for a celebration! Front row: John, Michael and Henry. Back row: on left could be Donald Walden with Ben. 1980

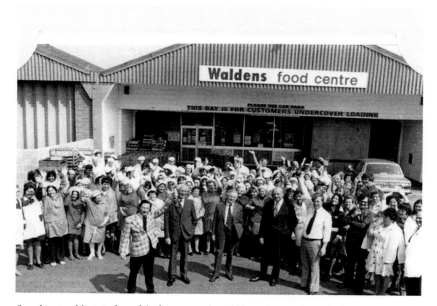

Something to celebrate in front of the first supermarket, which was later run by Michael Walden. In the front row are John, Donald and Henry Walden, Geoffrey Norris and Ben. Charlie Davis is far right. Perhaps Michael took the photo from above, he had a pilot's licence! (The cause for celebration was that we had obtained planning permission for the supermarket.)

Chapter 11). The name Frigfreight was chosen for being slightly French, as I had it in mind that the business could extend into continental Europe, bearing in mind that Britain was in the process of joining the European Common Market. The fact that the vehicles were carrying products for several frozen food manufacturers was a big advantage. Gradually Frigfreight was able to offer a weekly nationwide distribution service, which was exactly what the frozen pie business as well as several frozen food producers required.

Around this time, another milestone occurred which had a very important bearing on the future of Waldens. As our fleet of refrigerated vehicles increased, so did the requirement for diesel fuel. This attracted the attention of the major oil companies. I negotiated the best terms with Shell. Their representative happened to be Geoffrey Rice, ex RAF,

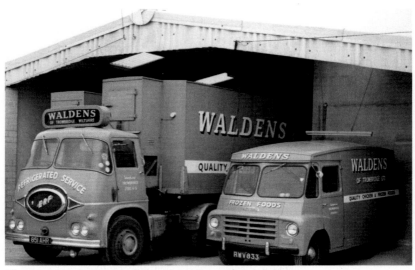

The original fleet of refrigerated vehicles parked in front of No 1 Cold Store

One of the fleet of 20 refrigerated vehicles operated by Frigfreight Ltd providing nationwide deliveries

Some of the 'fleet' parked in front of Cold Store No 2, about 1978

who had taken part as a pilot in the famous Dambusters raid in WW2 and many other operations.

One day a rep from the Regent Oil Company called to see if he could get our business. I told him I was already committed, but that Waldens had a site which could well be suitable as a petrol station. This was our factory on the Down, which was steadily becoming obsolete through the dominance of the supermarkets. That side of the business was losing money. Also having two sites meant there was a large measure of duplication of costs, heating, rates, labour, maintenance etc. The Regent Oil man indicated that his company was on the lookout for additional sites and said they would do a survey of the area to see if the site would be suitable. Apparently this was a matter of counting the chimney pots in the locality!

It took them two weeks to do the counting. Then he came back to see me and offered £36,000 for the site. I reported the offer to my father, and we very quickly accepted. Almost overnight, we closed the factory on the Down, discontinued making cakes etc., and moved everything to Ladydown. Many of the staff moved with us, although quite a few left, particularly the bakers who made the cakes. Freezing cakes was not practical, mainly because of the high sugar content and the delicate nature of the products. The knowledge we had gained, however, was soon applied to making puddings.

The butter factory, which was Henry's and Ben's baby, was moved to Ladydown and continued for several years. The unexpected influx of capital, probably worth £200,000 in today's currency, gave Waldens the chance to invest in new equipment which had, by then, become vital.

The frozen pie business progressed steadily and required new, faster machines. During this period my elder son, Hugh, who had completed his studies at both Portsmouth and Plymouth University, had joined the firm. Hugh had a flair for engineering. Ben recognised his talents and after a short time appointed him as Chief engineer. Ben purchased a

Waldens factory on The Down being demolished. Photo: Wiltshire Times, 1967. Quite sad!

large well-used second-hand high-volume Mateline pie-making machine and expected Hugh to refurbish it like new. This was impossible. Hugh did his best, but the machine was in very poor shape and he gave up. Ben had to employ an expensive specialist engineer and eventually, at great cost, they got the machine working. It would have been far cheaper - and more profitable - to have bought a new one!

This put Hugh off from working with his uncle. He left and enrolled at the International Boat Building College at Lowestoft, where he was able to develop his undoubted talents. Luckily, Ben and Hugh didn't fall out over this impasse and have remained on good terms ever since.

I concentrated on establishing contact with and appointing Frozen Food Wholesalers throughout the UK to ensure that retailers could be guaranteed a regular supply of our frozen products, mainly a wide range of Frozen Pies, Sausage Rolls etc. I engaged two Salesmen; Peter Ainsworth in the London area and Bill Clark in the North. Peter proved to be a great asset but, unfortunately, Bill was not successful. I established the business in the North myself with the help of Brother Michael for a short period. The volume steadily increased and the business was profitable.

During one trip to the Nottingham and Derby area I stayed at a quite special hotel in the Derbyshire Dales. Who should be among my fellow guests but the English World Cup football squad, headed by Sir Alf Ramsey, Brian Clough and Bobby Moore! Had I been less shy and a bit more streetwise I should have asked them for their autographs, which today would be quite valuable. Generally, I am not a football fan, preferring rugby and steeplechasing. However, in my younger days, just before WW2, I was a great fan of Sir Stanley Mathews CBE, who played for England, Stoke City and Blackpool (not all at the same time!) In his day he was regarded as the best in the world. Stan Matthews was the only player to be knighted whilst still playing and this was richly deserved. He was a genius and was still playing at the top level until he was 50!

Around this time we experimented with frozen meals for vending machines. We were ahead of our time, as vending machines and microwaves were not yet developed sufficiently for this project. A limited number of meals were sold to the RAF for inflight feeding, and the experience gained was soon to prove extremely valuable. Shortly afterwards, I had a stroke of luck, another one! Although I had no idea

Stanley Matthews in action

where it would lead, this eventually proved to be the making of the Walden business.

Out of the blue I had a phone call from Mrs Ruth Cotton, who lived in Cumbria. Ruth was the President of the local WRVS, based in Carlisle. She had grown up in Wiltshire and was aware of Waldens' activities in the frozen food industry. Ruth was the daughter of Richard Stratton, who farmed at Kingston Deverill near Warminster and was Chairman of the Wiltshire War Ag Committee during WW2.

Cumbria was, and still is, a very sparsely populated county consisting mostly of mountains and sheep. The WRVS was responsible for quite a number of day centres for the elderly, which were spread all over the entire county. Ruth Cotton was experiencing great difficulty in providing a reliable supply of quality meals to keep her clients well-nourished and happy. She had approached the right man to help her solve the problem!

Ruth advised me that she was about to visit her relatives in Wiltshire shortly and asked if she could come and see me. When we met, she explained that she wanted a good selection of high-quality meals and puddings and I agreed to prepare some menus to provide a different meal for each day of the week. This was quickly done, and with Ben's help in the factory, we set to work. In about ten days the first consignment was ready.

Cumbria is a long way from Trowbridge, over 300 miles, and it

Ruth Cotton MBE, President of the Cumbria WRVS. Ruth was the first person in the UK to use Waldens' frozen meals for feeding the elderly people in day centres across Cumbria. A real pioneer.

was obvious that it would be uneconomical to send a small van that distance. Ben did his best to persuade me to drop the idea. He was a bit short sighted, to say the least. My view was that this would be a 'trial run' and if it proved to be successful I was convinced that other similar and bigger organisations would be interested. This was soon to be proved correct!

The trial run in Cumbria, apart from costing a stack of money, was as I had predicted a great success. Our frozen pies were selling well all over the country, largely because 'I got on my bike' as Lord Tebbit famously once said and also that we had the means of distribution. Had I sat on my backside in my office in Trowbridge, Waldens would not have become the successful enterprise which it undoubtedly became.

I now set about making the frozen meal business into a major concern. To overcome the delivery problem to Cumbria I was able to find a local frozen food wholesaler who would stock our products and deal with the local distribution. This was the method I gradually established throughout England and Wales.

In London, my very capable salesman, Peter Ainsworth was well established. I believe he had been selling products to fish and chip shops before selling frozen pies for Waldens. I now asked him to scour the London Boroughs and see if he could generate any interest in our new products. By this time we had added bulk portion items, including main course and puddings (roughly 12 portions packed in foil trays), as well as the individual meals.

Peter, who knew London like the back of his hand, set to enthusiastically. One of his first ports of call was the Borough of Wandsworth, where he met the Supplies Officer, Fred Poynter. Many of the London Boroughs, and other municipal authorities all around the UK, were experiencing a problem in feeding their ever-increasing numbers of elderly people. Wandsworth was no exception and Peter was welcomed with open arms.

*Peter Ainsworth (left)
at an exhibition with
Michael Walden and an
attractive saleslady.*

Peter phoned me and said, 'John, you'd better come and see Fred ASAP'. I responded positively. At that time there were still many empty spaces around London which had not been redeveloped since the Blitz. One such area was by the Hammersmith Flyover at Brentford. I arranged to meet Peter there and he chauffeured me to Wandsworth. This became our regular meeting place and for a long time I travelled to London almost fortnightly. There was a lot of business to be done. Peter and I were a good team.

We duly met Fred and had an extremely productive session with him. In fact, Fred and his wife Rene became great friends of my wife Ann and me. (See Chapters 15 and 17)

Fred Poynter, Chief Supplies Officer for the London Borough of Wandsworth and the first major customer for Waldens Frozen Meals. Like Ruth Cotton, Fred was a pioneer.

We emerged from his office with an order, wait for it, for 9,000 meals and 9,000 sweets per week (each week!) When I announced this back in Trowbridge, the reaction was one of almost disbelief, impossible! Once it had registered, the question was how could this possibly be fulfilled?

It was a question of 'all hands on deck'. Ben, who by this time was in charge of production, together with his capable team, got cracking and the first order was delivered on time. It was quite a struggle but gradually the factory was steadily mechanized and better freezing plant was installed. Soon, liquid nitrogen freezing was introduced. This was supplied by Air Products and as it was a continuous process, it was a great step forward. In time it was used for freezing both meals and pies.

Gordon Read was Ben's right hand man and was responsible for all the purchasing and costing. This was a very important task which he did extremely well. Ben organised a vegetable preparation set up at Steeple Ashton separately to the business. He should have done it as part of the main business. However, it worked very well and ensured that the factory had a regular supply of good fresh veg. Ready-peeled potatoes were brought in from another local supplier. Fresh meat came from local suppliers too. Ben's chief chef at this time was Michael Love, while Phillip Yates ran the pie factory.

In the extremely severe winter of 1963, when the temperature in Trowbridge dropped to minus 18C, it quickly became impossible to obtain fresh vegetables for the meal business. All the crops were frozen in the ground. At this time I had several vehicles with 40ft refrigerated trailers, and at least three of these had just delivered their loads in the north of England. I immediately contacted one of my transport customers, J S Frozen Foods Ltd, who were large producers of frozen veg, mainly peas, runner and whole beans and sprouts. I persuaded them to load two of my trucks from their cold store in Lincolnshire and 40 tons of veg were brought back to Trowbridge. This kept the factory

Cold Stores 2 and 3 before the name
'WALDENS' was painted on the right-hand end

The name being painted over some years later

A pudding production line

going until fresh vegetables became available several weeks later. Once again, the value of our haulage business was demonstrated.

Peter Ainsworth continued his search for customers in London and when possible, I looked elsewhere. I succeeded in getting orders from Liverpool Corporation and Bristol, among others. Peter added the London Boroughs of Lambeth and Hammersmith quite quickly and others followed in due course. I established a base in the car park, which I used when I went to London, for our trucks. This was necessary as it was generally impossible for the drivers to deliver their complete loads in their permitted driving hours. I provided them with a static caravan for them to sleep in and this worked satisfactorily (this caravan is shown in the photo of the Walden site in Ladydown, above. It was being prepared to take to Brentford as accommodation for the drivers).

Back in Trowbridge, things were developing at quite a pace. On the administration side my cousin Donald FCA, who had worked with me in the poultry business, had returned to the fold after a spell with the Ross Group and became the Company Accountant. Donald produced monthly profit and loss figures for all our companies. This was vitally important. One particular month all three companies each made substantial profits. This was a good excuse for a celebration, which we arranged at a super restaurant, Beechfield House at Beanacre, near Melksham.

Following the closure of the factory on the Down, Geoffrey Norris, the Company Secretary, moved to Ladydown and continued in that capacity doing an excellent job. Waldens had a wonderful group of employees. Another one I must mention is Dennis Gerrish, who kept our fleet of vehicles in very good running order (see Chapter 11, Frigfreight).

The business soon outgrew the original cold store which I had built, which was no longer fit for purpose. Throughout this whole period of expansion a local building surveyor, Michael Dolman, was very much

Ben, John, Henry and Michael (photo taken at Beechfield)

involved with the design of the buildings, especially the cold stores. Brian Carpenter was also very much involved as the company's Chief Refrigeration and Electrical Engineer (See Chapter 11, Frigfreight Ltd.)

A much larger one was called for, and this needed considerable capital, which we didn't have. We approached ICFC, a venture capital company based in Bristol, and Donald and I went to see them. ICFC viewed our proposal positively and shortly advised us that they would loan the company £750,000. I went ahead and designed a palletised cold store. This included a loading bay at lorry tailboard height, whereas the storage area was at ground level. Movement of pallets within the store was by fork lift trucks, which placed the pallets on to the loading bay. All the loads on the artic trailers were on pallets. In time we grew out of this store and in about 1980 a further slightly larger cold store was added. This one used electric motors to open and close the pallet

Michael Dolman. A great help with designing buildings over many years.

isles which gave additional space, and it was designed so that it could use the existing loading bay. John Jones managed the cold stores for a long period. Later a retired Army Major, Bob Aitkenhead, took on the task. Stock keeping was a major task and he was particularly good at this.

By 1987 I had completed 35 years with the company. Major changes were being made and I felt that I had done my stint. Donald felt the same, and we both retired. My younger brother Ben took over and he continued to build successfully on the foundations which Father, Donald and I had established. One of Ben's most notable achievements was to establish franchise operators to sell the meals in their locality all over the country. This was a major improvement, as several of the wholesalers we had been supplying proved to be unreliable. When I retired Waldens were employing 650 people at Ladydown.

John Jones' retirement presentation. MHW, Margaret Jones, JW and John Jones.

Bob Aitkenhead, Cold Store Manager, 1980

My father Henry sadly passed away in 1983. During his life he had kept the peace between the three brothers. Without his steadying influence matters deteriorated and I, for one, greatly missed him. In due course Ben sold the business to the German firm apetito, which now sells the frozen meals as Wiltshire Farm Foods and employs over 1200 people. I understand that they are also established in Canada. They produce frozen meals in Germany, Holland and France. To get over the staff problem, I am told that they fly in a load of workers from Poland, who rotate with others on a regular basis. (See www.apetito.co.uk, which records when they acquired Waldens - see also Wikipedia re apetito).

We three brothers all contributed in different ways to the success of Waldens. Personally I am very proud of my involvement in the firm and particularly of the fact that we employed so many local people. Over the years it would be thousands, and I am sure that like me, they enjoyed working for Waldens. Only one point, as I write these pages, disappoints me, and that is that after the 70 years in which the Walden family were in business in Trowbridge there is practically no recognition of the fact

Waldens used to bus the staff in and out, apetito fly them!

that we existed or of how much Trowbridge owes to us and our staff, except for a minor mention in Trowbridge Museum. I hope that my book will fill a gap.

The following document was issued or sanctioned by Ben Walden at about the time the business was sold to apetito. Ben was under the impression that when the sale was completed, he would be the CEO of apetito in the UK. About two years after the sale was completed Ben agreed to retire. You will note that there is no mention of Ben's two brothers, John and Michael.

Ronnie Corbett: Top class 'chef' and the best salesman apetito will ever find!

Dennis Gerrish, just before his 90th birthday, finally hangs up his spanners after completing nearly 60 years of valuable service to the Walden and apetito companies. The occasion was marked by a lunch on the 23rd December 2014. With Dennis is Paul Freeston CEO of apetito, who made a presentation.

From left: Dennis Walters MP, Collin White, Eileen Lucas, Ben Walden, Dennis Gerrish, Sylvia Escott and Ray Ward. Photo taken on the occasion of a long service celebration. Collin White was my first Cold Store Manager. Ray Ward joined Waldens in about 1936 as a van salesman. Dennis has completed 60 years with the firm and in 2014 he is in good shape at the ripe old age of 90. Photo 1988

John Walden, 2009

The last member of the Walden family in the family business, Ben, Chairman from 1981 until the company was sold in 1996. He worked with the new owners for the following two years and then retired.

Historical Development

Wiltshire Farm Foods Limited is a sister company of Waldens Wiltshire Foods. The business was founded in Trowbridge by the grandfather and father of the current Chairman, Mr Ben Walden.

Herbert Walden and his son, Henry Walden, laid the foundations of the business in 1928. It was their foresight and motivation which set Waldens on the right course. Henry Walden's entrepreneurial spirit has continued through the family, and now his son leads Waldens as we know it today.

The company started as Waldens Mid-Wilts Creameries. In a factory close to our present site in Trowbridge they ran a butter-packing operation. As this business expanded and contacts with local farmers flourished, Waldens started selling eggs and meat and manufacturing pies and sausages.

After the war came a change of name to Waldens of Trowbridge. The company diversified and began manufacturing cakes and pastries while operating a van sales network throughout the south of England. This continued well into the late '60s. It was then that the frozen food revolution was beginning. At this time, Waldens Wiltshire Foods, as it became known, started to manufacture frozen unbaked pies and ready meals. It very soon became a national supplier of the products, produced from locally-supplied ingredients.

By the middle of the 70s, Waldens was established on its present ten-acre site, where it had its production factory, cold storage facility and one of its three supermarkets. The 'Food Centres', in three West Country towns, were opened as a result of demand for the products produced in Trowbridge. By the late 80s, the supermarkets had grown and established themselves to such a degree that they were sold to a supermarket chain based in Devon.

Today Waldens Wiltshire Foods and Wiltshire Farm Foods together specialise in the manufacture and sale of frozen products to the rapidly-growing welfare market. From its roots back in 1928, Waldens now has its eyes set firmly on the future with the family enterprise, passed on to the Chairman, Mr Ben Walden, still very much alive.

CHAPTER 11

FRIGFREIGHT LTD, REFRIGERATED ROAD HAULAGE

Nationwide distribution

As my venture into the frozen food business became established, I set about developing a refrigerated transport business. This would have been in about 1964. After the end of WW2 the socialist government had nationalized practically all road transport. Like most nationalized outfits, this was a disaster. Fortunately, the majority of the most left-wing MPs were not re-elected in a subsequent election, when Winston Churchill was returned as Prime Minister. Churchill was a great supporter of free enterprise, as I am. Gradually most of the sectors which had been nationalized were returned to private ownership and this included road transport, which had been run as British Road Services, and of course much later, British Rail.

At that time it was necessary to apply for a licence to operate a road transport business. Many of the original operators had managed to get their businesses back and by the time I entered this sector they were well established. They had formed the Road Haulage Association (RHA) and one of its main objectives was to protect its members' businesses. I had to apply for a licence at the Department of Transport (DoT) in Bristol and this application was circulated to all members. The local members had a branch in Devizes and they lodged an objection to my application. This resulted in a hearing before the DoT and the RHA, which I was summoned to attend. It was a very serious matter and I made enquiries as to who might represent me at the hearing.

My very good friend and solicitor (and one time neighbour) Tony King (see Chapters 2, 13 and 17) of Sylvester and Mackett of Trowbridge, recommended Max Macgregor-Johnson of Wansbroughs, solicitors, Devizes. I duly made an appointment to see Max. He was precisely the right man for the job. It was his specialty and I would say there was none better. Max's son Stuart, at the time of writing this story, is the Senior Partner in Wansbroughs, which is one of the largest and best practices in the West of England.

Max advised that it would be pointless to apply for several vehicles at one time. It was a question of 'softly softly catchee monkey', and this was the approach we adopted. We applied for two vehicles to begin with. Max represented me at the hearing and the objections were quite forceful. In the end, I believe we only succeeded in getting a licence for one vehicle, and this was restricted to a radius of 100 miles, plus some other unhelpful restrictions. The opposition were quite determined to keep me out if they could. Quite frankly it was barely worth having the licence for one vehicle, but it was a start.

Some time later, I applied to join the RHA. If you can't beat them, join them! By this time the members had decided that I wasn't a huge threat to their livelihoods, primarily because I was only aiming to carry frozen products, which didn't compete with their activities. I was accepted and attended their regular meetings in Devizes and got to know many of them quite well.

Among those who had originally objected were Syms Transport at Calne, SCC Transport, Frank Chivers and Son and G Pearce and Sons, all based in Devizes; Forseys of Weston Super Mare; Carpenter and Son, of Crudwell; and G T Brown of Steeple Ashton. Chivers, Carpenters and Browns are still in business today and most of them, especially Browns, would have been, for at least three generations, beginning with the horse and cart!

My future applications were accepted without opposition. Gradually I found more and more business and added more trucks, which eventually numbered about 20, including six artics with 40ft trailers, all with mechanical refrigeration and well-insulated bodies. After about five years or so, the licensing procedure was abolished. It is now possible for anyone to operate a transport business provided they have certain experience and qualifications, especially in relation to road safety. Legislation has now been introduced aimed at improving the standards of maintenance to make vehicles safer and Department of Transport

My first artic tractor and trailer. Underpowered, but it was a start! The refrigeration unit on this container was one of the first to be fitted to a road vehicle. Prior to this, blocks of cardice, supplied by ICI, were used (see Chapter 8)

Testing Stations were established nationwide. The nearest one to Trowbridge was at Calne, which was, and is, a very efficient set up.

Opposite our establishment in Canal Road there had been the Wyke Brick and Tile Company Brickworks, previously owned by Alfie Crease. This had now become the southern depot for Carmen's Transport (Later to trade as Brit-European Transport) and I got to know the Depot Manager. I picked his brains with regard to the most suitable tractors to buy. He advocated ERF tractors with Gardner engines. He thought a five-cylinder engine would be suitable to begin with, but this proved to be quite wrong. The vehicle was very good but the engine was not fit for purpose – it was underpowered.

Bearing in mind the dubious advice I had been given, the first tractor I purchased was a British-built ERF with a five-cylinder Gardner engine. To couple up to this tractor I bought two 24-foot trailers, a 'special offer' from Taskers, trailer makers, of Andover. They had been made for use in Switzerland and were designed for use where there were many sharp bends in the mountainous terrain. They were extremely well-made and were fitted with rear wheel steering, which is widely used nowadays. They arrived as 'flatbeds'. Our very skilled carpenter/joiner/patternmaker, Archie Bennett, built the Insulated containers and Dennis Gerrish, our Chief Motor Mechanic (later Garage Manager) carried out all the metalwork, both internal and external. The insulation, at that time, was first class and they were built to last. Dennis sprayed both of them in the open air!

Dennis Gerrish. The right-hand photo was taken shortly after Dennis joined Waldens in 1954. 90% of the land was still pasture, grazed by cattle. In 2014 the whole area has become the Canal Road Industrial Estate, which was started by the Walden family. The left-hand photo shows Dennis working (or having fun!) on a British Leyland vehicle in the firm's workshop, 2005.

Dennis joined Waldens at the age of thirty in 1954, shortly after the new garage was built at Ladydown; Fred Rolfe was in charge at that time. Later, when commercial vehicle testing became law in 1962, Dennis, now in charge, made it clear to his staff that it was his aim to ensure that every vehicle taken to be tested had to be 100% roadworthy so that it passed the test first time. Tests were carried out at the Department of Transport Testing Station at Calne. Annual tests are compulsory. The scheme has vastly improved the safety of road transport and minimized costly breakdowns for those engaged in the Industry.

In the 30 or more years following the introduction of vehicle testing, Dennis and his capable staff sent 109 vehicles to be tested and, without exception, they all passed first time. This must be a record, as I know that many vehicles from other firms frequently failed the test. Well done Dennis! I am sure the standard set by Dennis, and maintained over the years, made a huge contribution to the success not only of Frigfreight but also of the Walden Group as a whole.

Another point I must mention is the very important role which my cousin Donald, our superb accountant, played in the development and success of Frigfreight. Because of the professional way the accounting side of the business was dealt with, Donald was able to arrange finance for practically all the vehicles we purchased, mainly on 2 or 3-year term hire purchase. All HP agreements were honoured in full.

One of the early loads carried by the first artic unit was driven by Brian Randall. He had a full load destined for Cornwall, and somewhere in Devon he came to a pretty steep hill. Part way up the engine snuffed it - it wasn't powerful enough. This was a serious setback. I had to send a smaller vehicle to lighten the load. We made sure we didn't overload this tractor in future.

Not very long after the episode in Devon, there was an extremely tragic incident in Hilperton, where Brian Randall lived. Poor Brian, who was a very decent fellow, became involved in a serious dispute between his daughter and her boyfriend. The tragic outcome was that both Brian and his daughter were murdered and the boyfriend killed himself. A sad and messy end, especially for Brian's mother, who also worked for Waldens.

Progress! Artic unit No 2 with Seddon tractor fitted with an 8-cylinder Gardner engine and an alloy container body. This vehicle hit its roof off under a low bridge in South Wales. Never a dull moment! At least one other vehicle suffered the same problem. Fortunately most bridges have been improved in recent years. Another one, a 7 tonner, failed to slow down as it approached a Roundabout being constructed near Chippenham to cross the M4 Motorway. It landed in the middle! It was early morning and I believe that the driver had "dropped off". Luckily he was not seriously hurt.

Gardner engines were recognized as the best in the world at that time. They would go for years and years with minimal problems, and over 300,000 miles on the clock was quite normal before any major repair was needed. I investigated other British makes of tractors with much more powerful 8 cylinder Gardner engines. Seddon was one make which I bought, and another was Atkinson. These two makes soon merged to become Seddon-Atkinson. Gradually I had a mixed fleet, all with Gardner engines except one, which had a Rolls Royce engine, about eight tractors with about 10 x 40 ft trailers which, of course, are interchangeable and allow for preloading. Apart from these I had about 10 7-tonners, mostly British Leyland, which were not as reliable as the tractors with Gardner engines but they did their job.

Over the years the fleet steadily increased, and when possible we made sure that the artic tractors were fitted with Gardner engines. There was a gap when Gardner had a prolonged strike and Rolls Royce Eagle engines had to be used. In a recent discussion with Dennis Gerrish, now aged 90 and still going strong, I was told that the RR engines not only used more fuel, but water (with Blue Glycol antifreeze) found its way into the oil and ended up in the sump and that the fuel pumps too were unreliable. This was reported to RR and no doubt they made appropriate modifications. When possible we stuck to Gardner's, which gave outstanding reliability. Due to this, they were widely used all over the world both in boats and trucks, and many are still running to this day. Later American Cummings engines gradually replaced them. Perkins diesel engines, which were made in Peterborough, were, and are, fitted to many smaller vehicles and lots of boats. These have proved to be very reliable too.

When Frigfreight was launched, the Garage was well-equipped and Dennis was joined by Tom Bennett (ex REME). As a point of interest for any youngster who is contemplating a career in motor engineering, the training given in the Royal Mechanical and Electrical engineers is probably the best you can get and it costs nothing! The mechanical refrigeration units on each vehicle required regular servicing and we employed several skilled refrigeration engineers, initially headed by Brian Carpenter, who had been with Waldens as Chief Electrician for many years. His son Howard followed in his father's footsteps and his younger son Julian now runs their refrigeration business, which Brian established when he retired from Waldens.

Brian Carpenter, retired and on holiday. Brian was the Chief Electrical and Refrigeration Engineer for the Walden Group for many years.

Left: John Maynard, Traffic Manager in the Transport office. Right: Richard Ledbury, Transport Manager, 1980

As the frozen food business developed the point was soon reached when I had to delegate some of my duties. A transport manager was needed, and it required someone with experience in the transport business. I was fortunate in finding Richard Ledbury, who had been working in the Transport Department of Unigate, whose head office, at that time, was in Trowbridge. He was familiar with all the legal requirements, which were becoming increasingly complex and important. He was also used to dealing with customers. Richard was just what was needed and he was a great help to me. We worked together for about 15 years. Unfortunately Richard was addicted to smoking small cigars, dozens per day and, slowly, this affected his health. He died at the early age of 40.

A new artic and 40ft trailer unit with Richard Ledbury in the cab and JW next to it. Most of the tractors had sleeper cabs.

Atkinson tractor with a Rolls-Royce engine. Not as good as the Gardner engines. Trailer in Flying Goose livery (Danmaid Seafood)

A later version of the Danmaid livery

Pride of the fleet!

Frigfreight - delivering countrywide

One of my star drivers, Jock Wallis, preparing to mount a container on to a Leyland truck. Interchangeable bodies like trailers, facilitate preloading, which is a great advantage.

Tony Trotman's rally car, sponsored by Waldens. Left to right: Michael, Ben, Henry and John.

Frigfreight had a very professional set-up. Fit for purpose! This fully came to the fore in the in the very severe winter of 1963. On a particular Monday morning the temperature in Trowbridge fell to -18 C, possibly the lowest on record. The diesel froze in all the vehicles. Urgent action was needed. Dennis conferred with Richard Ledbury, who did some quick research and found that by diluting the diesel with paraffin this would solve the problem. Dennis organized the paraffin and by 10 am that morning all the vehicles were on the road. Providing the firm paid the duty on the amount of paraffin used this was within the law! Nowadays, (2014) winter diesel for low temperatures is available.

We used the spell of bad weather; it lasted from early March until the middle of April, to our advantage. Many haulage firms had much worse problems than we did, especially those involved in collecting milk from Farms. Even a few miles from Trowbridge the narrow lanes were blocked with 3 or 4 feet of snow for weeks on end. A lot of milk was wasted through lack of collection and poured down the drain. Fresh vegetables were non-existent, frozen in the ground. There was, however, plenty of frozen in cold stores in Lincolnshire. We loaded back many loads. This proved to be vital for Waldens as it enabled them to maintain production of Frozen Meals without a break. In addition we kept several frozen food wholesalers in the south of England and South Wales supplied.

Among the Customers Frigfreight served were Flying Goose, who handled increasing amounts of frozen seafood. This was founded by a Dane, Piers Jensen, in Sutton Veney. As the business prospered larger premises were acquired in Warminster. Some of the success of Flying Goose can be attributed to the good service which Frigfreight provided as they were able to take advantage of the established nationwide service fully utilized by Waldens Wiltshire Foods Ltd. Later Flying Goose sold out to Lyons Seafood, which is a substantial player in the seafood business in 2014, still operating in the Warminster area. Arthur Shering (Director and General Manager), Keith Stone, Jim Johnson (both sales), David Ridout (Factory Manager) and David Pitkethley (Transport Manager) were the principle members of the Flying Goose Team.

Union International was regular bulk customer. We regularly collected frozen fish from South Africa from Union Castle ships which docked at Avonmouth and Southampton. The loads were delivered to Union cold stores wherever they were required. McCain Frozen Chips, and Iddiens of Worcester, who handle vast quantities of Black Currants were regulars. Among others was Henley-in-Arden Ice Cream.

Loads of frozen vegetables were transported from cold stores in Lincolnshire, which was and is, the main producing area in the UK for a wide range of veg including peas, sprouts, cauliflower and broccoli. Quite early on I obtained a Class 1 Heavy Goods Driving Licence. In the event of a driver being taken ill I would step in and do the job.

It is fairly obvious that it is advantageous to keep vehicles loaded with both outward and return loads. This is something that Richard and I did our best to develop, with a good degree of success. It definitely contributed to the profit that Frigfreight made. Waldens' butter business was managed at this time by Michael Marsh under the direction of brother Ben. Butter was an expensive commodity. Frigfreight regularly took loads of frozen food, including Waldens' products, to Devon and Cornwall. The butter company purchased many tons of butter from a dairy in Cornwall and used Peter Green Transport to bring it to Trowbridge. I approached Marsh and Ben to see if Frigfreight could do the job at the going rate or slightly less. The answer was no. There was no obvious reason for this refusal, as Frigfreight was owned by the Walden Group of Companies.

Shortly, and quite out of the blue, the reason became apparent. One of Peter Green's trucks had been spotted by an observant woman as it was leaving the Cornish dairy bound for Waldens' butter factory at Ladydown. She noted that the trailer's body was practically touching the tyres and was obviously substantially overloaded. She called the police and the vehicle was pulled over. It was quickly found that the driver and someone else at the dairy had overloaded the vehicle by two tons!

The driver, or someone, must have informed the police that Michael Marsh was also involved in this 'great butter robbery'. It had been noticeable that for some time Marsh had been driving a quite expensive BMW and had a mistress, which prompted the view that he was living beyond his 'legal' means.

Marsh was interviewed by Trowbridge Police, but before there was an opportunity of establishing the full facts and background to this episode, he took his own life. Later, while I was doing some 'research', I was told he had been 'trading' in butter separately to running the Waldens' butter business. I guess he was a dubious individual and not a loyal employee of Waldens.

Among my drivers, two stand out, Monty Knight and Jock Wallis. Monty preferred the longer trips, including the run to Scotland. He used to leave Trowbridge around 4 am or before and would make a number of deliveries on the way north. Richard Ledbury made sure that he had a return load where possible. One of the companies we hauled for was McCain's, and often they would have a load of chips coming south. On one occasion Monty got involved with a McCain loader and loaded more chips than he should have done. Somehow he got caught trying to sell them for cash.

Having been informed, I had to decide what to do with Monty. In the normal course of events it would be instant dismissal, but in the case of Monty, who had been with me for many years, this was something I would avoid if I could. I had him in the office and read him the riot act. Monty was ashamed of himself. The outcome was that I gave him another chance, and he never let me down again.

Jock Wallis was another stalwart. Sometime after my retirement, Monty died suddenly and Jock rang me to see if I would go to his funeral. I did. After the funeral, Jock came up to me and said I was the best boss in Trowbridge, which I appreciated. I think he meant it and I agreed! Three other drivers I remember were Ian Currie (who moved to Airsprung), Mike Pratt and Alan Walker.

Monty Knight; left and above. In addition to the 40 ft articulated trailers we used a number of trailers such as the one above. This unit would carry a larger payload than the 40ft trailers and the vehicle can be used with or without the trailer. Quite versatile!

One thing which I introduced was a new method of paying the drivers. If they were paid overtime, some were known to drag out their hours, probably parking up in a layby. I thought of a way to prevent this. They were paid quite a high basic wage plus a substantial unsocial hour payment for all hours worked before 7 am. This did the trick!

Frigfreight container mounted on a Crane Fruehauf trailer. Note letters TIR. This stands for Transport International Routier and was a legal requirement for European operations prior to the advent of the Common Market, which now allows for free movement of member countries vehicles crossing borders.

Throughout my business life, 99% of my ideas and efforts have proved to be successful. There was one, however, which was seen to be worthwhile pursuing, but failed through the inadequacies of another person (and me!) My idea was to sell frozen vegetables for a third party and arrange for Frigfreight to deliver the products to the customer. This would provide additional work for Frigfreight and increase its revenue and profitability. To this end I formed a limited company called Minus 20 (standing for minus 20 Centigrade, the temperature for the storage and carriage of frozen food). A previous frozen pie customer of mine, Doug Cantwell, who had recently moved to Trowbridge, paid me a call to see if I had a job for him. I immediately decided, too quickly, that he could be the salesman for Minus 20, and he jumped at the idea.

The main supplier which I had agreed to sell products for was JS Frozen Foods Ltd (JSFF) from Lincolnshire. Minus 20 were to get the orders, which were to be invoiced by JSFF, who would collect the monies for their goods. Frigfreight would make the deliveries, for which they would charge 1/2p per lb. Doug Cantwell, who was quite well known in the frozen food trade, very quickly sent in some useful orders and Frigfreight duly made the deliveries.

Unfortunately, a number of Doug Cantwell's customers turned out to be 'dodgy' and deliberately ordered large quantities of products for which they had no intention of paying. He took the orders and neither he, nor JSFF, carried out a credit check. I had assumed that Doug would be dealing with genuine companies. Very quickly JSFF put a stop on supplying Minus 20 customers. The only way they would do business was for Minus 20 to purchase the products and sell them on. This was something I was not prepared, or organized, to do, particularly bearing in mind the disastrous experience I had had so far. Minus 20 was soon wound up. This idea would have worked if the salesman had sold to genuine buyers. The best customer Minus 20 had was Waldens, who bought many tons of veg for which they paid, especially during the extremely cold winter of 1963. It was worth a try!

Before I retired I investigated the possibility of establishing an underground cold store. I had discovered somewhere that the Swedes had constructed one or more cold stores in mountains. I paid a visit to Sweden and was shown one of their cold stores and was very impressed.

As many will know, Bath is surrounded by disused stone mines, probably at least six, and several are of special interest. The one at Westwood was used during WW2 to house the Crown Jewels, and one at Copenacre, west of Corsham, was used as the main storage unit for the Royal Navy. Between Corsham and Melksham is a massive mine known as Eastlays. During WW2 Eastlays was one of the largest ammunition dumps in the UK. It had its own railway siding, and 4000 men worked there and slept underground. Eastlays mine is so extensive that it links up with the Royal Navy stores at Copenacre on the other side of Corsham, three to four miles away!

Eastlays was the one which interested me. The Bath and Portland Stone Company, which was based in Bath, still had mining interests in the area, although not at Eastlays. I contacted them and they showed a definite interest in my ideas, which not only included cold storage but a possible HQ for Frigfreight Ltd, together with a base for their trucks. Together, there was great potential.

As the present method of moving products in and out of the mine was by a very steep conveyor, one of the ideas we considered was to open up the mine so that trucks could access it from the bottom of the mine. The temperature underground was a constant 40F. I arranged for our Chief Refrigeration Engineer at Waldens, Brian Carpenter, to carry out a feasibility test to establish the effect of freezing on the stone walls. Freezing did not affect the stone and a temperature of -20 C could be held with minimal cost. The mine was divided up into many quite large chambers which would be suitable for stacking pallets four high.

This proposition was reaching a point where work could have been started. At this time the Portland Stone Company (PSC) had many interests, including building the M1 Motorway. The boss happened to be Ernest Marples MP, Minister of Transport at that time. PSC also had a very large project on the go in Iran (known as Persia in those days) where they were also building motorways. Then a revolution developed in Iran, the Shah of Persia was deposed and the state took over everything. PSC had to beat a very hasty retreat, leaving behind masses of expensive road building equipment. This was a financial disaster for PSC and they were unable to invest in the Eastlays mine. Later the mine was developed and I believe it is now storing vast amounts of wine, for which it would be ideal.

CHAPTER 12

BLACKLAND LAKES HOLIDAY AND
LEISURE CENTRE, 1976-2014

When I purchased Knights Marsh Farm in 1971, I had a lot of help from Waldens drivers and a couple of Waldens vans to make the move from Great Hinton, about 12 miles away. At this time KMF had 73 acres of pasture. I was, at that time, fully employed by Waldens Wiltshire Foods Ltd in Trowbridge. Initially I grazed some cattle on the land and made hay. My main interest in purchasing the farm was to enable me to keep a couple of horses, but also to farm the land as much as time permitted.

Unfortunately 70 acres of the land was on the opposite side of a fairly busy lane, which was a drawback. If possible it is best to avoid crossing roads with animals. At the same time 70 acres was more land than I needed, so gradually I sold much of this land. I was aware that Dykes Farm, which was close by and included land adjoining the three acres on the right side of the road next to the farmhouse, was due to come on the market. I made contact with the auctioneers, Thompson Noad and Phipp of Chippenham, and spoke to Norman Addington, who was dealing with the sale. I was advised that the property was to be sold in three lots by auction, and one of the lots happened to be 15 acres which adjoined the three acres by KM Farmhouse. This would be ideal for my purpose. I attended the auction and bought it for £9000. I then set about selling the remainder of the 70 acres opposite. The buyer was David Tyler, who farmed at Heddington, close to the Ivy.

One of the first things which needed attention was the access from Stockley Lane, which was very dangerous as there was no visibility. Using a lot of rubble I set about making a new one on the Calne side of the Dutch barn, initially for one-way traffic. In those days you didn't consult the planners. It was common sense!

The new 15 acres was divided by Heddington Brook and the land at the lower end of the property was extremely wet, so much so that when chain harrowing, the tractor I was driving not only got stuck but sank above the rear axle. A neighbour's tractor just managed to get it out.

At this time, a Stan Haines was doing some building work for me, constructing cattle and sheep pens in the barn area by the road. We were using recycled material, mostly metal pipes. Stan took an interest in my predicament. Some years previously, he had been employed on the redevelopment of the severely flood-damaged villages of Lynton and Lynmouth in North Devon, Blackfords of Calne being the main contractors. During this work the driver of a dragline excavator walked off the job and Stan replaced him. Stan did such a good job that on completing the contract Mr Blackford gave him the machine, together with a large tractor and winch. The latter was a necessary part of the set up to ensure that the dragline could always be recovered! It was obvious that there was plenty of water in the area where I had been stuck and Stan, having had a lot of experience with this sort of problem, suggested that we should dig a hole about 20' x 20' and see what happened. I agreed, and he duly brought his machines and set to work.

It was quite exciting, as each bucketful of soil which Stan dug out was replaced with beautiful clean water which came gushing in. Within an hour or so we had a pond full of water. Water in the right place can be a useful asset, and this proved to be the case. I agreed to let Stan continue digging and I kept him at it for a year, during which time he dug out three useful size lakes between three quarters of an acre and one acre each. One of them I named Stan's Lake and for the first summer it was so clean that I and my family were swimming in it regularly.

Some of the material Stan extracted was chalky and very hard, so much so that the machine had difficulty in shifting it. A lot of it had leaf fossils, which indicated that it hadn't seen the light of day for millions of years. A Wessex Water geologist called and advised that this was 'tufa'. I made an attractive rockery with it.

Spring Lake with the ducks and, on the right a super carp weighing thirty pounds or more.

The 'Babbling Brook'   *Stan's Lake*

An aerator in use on Stan's Lake. In continuous hot weather the lakes can suffer with the problem of algae, which can cause de-oxygenation and seriously affect the fish and other pond life. A camping fisherman, John Bright (in the check shirt), is discussing the matter with Sam Walden.

The 15 acres I had purchased had been neglected for many years. I set to work to tidy it up. The hedges were as wide as a house. To suit my needs I divided the large fields into nine paddocks and planted hedges and hundreds of trees. Initially there was no access between KM Farmhouse and the 15 acres, and also there was only one bridge linking the land either side of Heddington Brook. The existing bridge must have been several hundred years old. It leaned at a precarious angle and to negotiate it with a load of hay was a work of art! I restored this bridge as soon as possible and added another one close to the farmhouse to give access to the land the other side of the brook.

This was in 1976, one of the hottest and driest summers on record. The brook had practically dried out and this was an ideal time to build a bridge. I decided to design and build it myself. With this in mind I engaged a couple of fellows to dig four holes 3 feet deep below the bottom of the dried-out brook. These were filled with concrete and then four block pillars were built on top to just below the bank. Each of these pillars was reinforced with angle iron, which protruded about six inches above, the purpose of which was to hold steel girders with which I proposed to span the brook.

I went to Drinkwater's in Trowbridge and bought two very heavy 20 feet long girders. These I brought home on a trailer towed by my Land Rover. The load was excessive, and going down Whetham Hill it was as much as I could do to prevent the trailer from jack-knifing. It was a close shave! It was also quite a performance, with a tractor and front end loader, getting the girders in position over the brook and lowering them on to the four pillars.

Once the girders were securely in place, railway crossing sleepers were laid across them and the bridge was ready for use. Thirty-eight years later the bridge is still in good shape and has since been covered with Tarmac. I often had 20-tonne loads cross it!

It was also necessary to make a road to the lower bridge to make it accessible in wet weather. This, of course gave access to the three lakes which Stan had made. Gradually I accomplished this using Mendip stone and scalpings and then a finer gravel, mostly purchased from Ross Hillman of Westbury. Tarmac was added later. I was quite proud of what I had achieved and organized an open day to show it off to the locals.

When I started this project I had had no idea that planning permission was required to make the three lakes or jumps for horses. Someone had obviously reported the development, because the morning after the open day an official-looking man appeared. He was an ex-policeman employed by North Wiltshire District Council as an enforcement officer. He was both obnoxious and overbearing. He said I had broken the law and threatened to arrest me there and then. I objected, and due to his unacceptable approach told him to get off my property. Afterwards I rang the Planning Department and told the lady planning officer what had transpired. She agreed that the enforcement officer had overstepped the mark and said she would come and see me the following morning.

Children making good use of the play area

JW being presented with the West Conservation Award by Prince Charles at the Royal Bath and West Show, 1987

The Blackland Lakes Open Day 1985, opened by the President of the World Wildlife Fund. The vehicle is a Volvo C150 4x4. The bridge had recently been re-built. Note horses taking an interest (Tornado and Dancer, see Chapter 15, In the Saddle).

The Planning Officer was most helpful and asked me what I would like planning permission for. This was very encouraging and my brain went into overdrive. Some time prior to this episode I had had a visit by my cousin Marion Brunt, from Faversham in Kent. Marion suggested that I should apply to the Camping and Caravan Club and/or the Caravan Club for a Certified Location, which was for a maximum of five units. By now this was already in place using an ex-Waldens van body fitted out with male and female facilities. Five units proved to be neither one thing nor the other, in fact, more of a nuisance. To exceed five units planning permission would be required. In addition to the three lakes and amongst other things of less importance, such as horse jumps, I applied for a proper caravan site, and this was granted. The permission stated that I could have 40 caravans during the summer and ten in the winter. This was a good start and I now built the first permanent toilet block. I preferred wooden buildings for the camp site, as they blended in well with the rural area.

After a nasty fire in the first building a second one was bought to house a reception and shop. This came on two trucks from M and M Timber in Shropshire, and was craned into place onto dwarf walls. No expensive concrete base! Later, in order to widen the access to the campsite, I was able to move the whole building by placing two RSJs (rigid steel joists) under them plus a spreader above (supplied by Hiscock engineers in Trowbridge). Devizes Cranes brought a crane which proved to be inadequate - it tipped over! A larger one did the job.

The fire referred to above was caused by an electrical fault. As I complete this book at the end of December 2014, news has just come through of a caravan fire in which two children and an adult have, tragically, lost their lives. Sometime in the 1980s I was present at Blackland Lakes when I spotted smoke and then flames emanating from a caravan which I happened to be approaching. I ran to the door and shouted to the occupants "Get out quick!" The couple, from Essex, I forget their name, got out in the nick of time. There was a violent explosion and the caravan burst into flames. It was a complete write off. This was a gas explosion. Great care is needed both in boats and caravans. (See Chapter 13, Boats and Boating, which has a passage about gas and paraffin cookers).

Duke of Edinburgh Award Scheme campers, plus ducks!

A Fire Pit, organized by Sam Walden for a group headed by Andrew and Charlotte Pardy in the summer of 2014. The turf is rolled back after use thus avoiding damage. Good idea Sam!

Alan Fletcher, good friend and Bank Manager (Midland Bank/HSBC). Alan organized funds to finance the building of Ablution Block 2, and later, the Health and Fitness Club, including the very special level deck swimming pool.

One of the new lakes (known as Heron Lake) was stocked with rainbow trout for fly fishing. This proved to be a mistake, as there was inadequate oxygen due to an insufficient flow of water. In addition I continually had to travel to West Lavington to replenish the stock. Before long, I restocked this and Stan's Lake with a good selection of coarse fish, carp, tench, roach and perch, and this is now very popular with local fishermen and holiday makers as well as the resident kingfishers and herons! Pike were not included in the stocking, but over the years a number have been caught. The pikes' eggs were most likely introduced by birds bringing them from elsewhere, possibly from the River Marden which runs through Calne or the Kennet and Avon Canal, which is not far away as the crow flies. In the third lake (Spring Lake) I added a collection of wildfowl, which became an interesting feature. The lakes attracted lots of wild ducks and geese and even the odd swan. Before I constructed the lakes it was quite rare to see any ducks at Knights Marsh Farm. Before long they were very plentiful and campers enjoyed feeding them. Kingfishers established themselves and were soon fishing with the fishermen! Further bridges had to be built. Electric hook-up points for caravans were installed, and water and waste points established, all costing a considerable amount of cash!

As my two sons became more independent, my wife Barbara was able to play a very important part in running the business. As it progressed the development was very much a joint effort. After my retirement from the business in 2007, Barbara and Sam, together with the able help of Rupert Crockett, who manages the Health and Fitness Club, have ensured that the business has gone from strength to strength. Other long service and very capable staff include Penny Slayton, the Chief Receptionist in the club, and Catherine Harrison, who manages the campsite reception and shop.

*Rupert Crockett, the
very able and pleasant
Manager of the
Blackland Leisure,
Health and Fitness
Club*

*JW holding a kingfisher rescued from the island in Stan's Lake. It had been caught on a fishermen's hook.
Luckily it wasn't hurt and flew away to continue fishing, at no charge! The rescuer jumped in and promptly
disappeared - he had to swim to the island. The depth was nearly nine feet. He had quite a shock!*

*The above photos shows one of the latest fresh and waste water installations designed and installed in each
camping paddock by Sam with advice from Wessex Water. These completely hygienic units ensure that the fresh
water is never contaminated. The bricks are available for campers to keep their barbecues from burning the grass.*

162

At the beginning of my involvement in the camping business I aimed for as many campers as possible. This resulted in overcrowding and was counterproductive. We cut the numbers down, and when Sam took over he marked out each pitch so that each caravan has an acceptable area. This has proved to be a great improvement.

The well-stocked shop and reception and No. 1 Ablution Block. Blackland Lakes is one of the most pleasant commercial campsites in the UK

In time, as more campers came to Blackland Lakes, I was able to obtain planning permission for an additional toilet block and extra caravans and tents. The entrance was modified to take two-way traffic and barriers were installed to provide security and to ensure that all visitors paid their dues. Eventually the business became viable and made a profit. It is now one of the most attractive commercial campsites in the UK. As I slowly took a back seat, my son Sam took on the manager's task and it is now better than ever. Before I retired, Sam and I, with the capable aid of Dave Weston, built a dam across Heddington Brook. This is a pleasant feature and reminds me of a 'babbling brook'.

Around 2000 'CombiPitches' were introduced. Caravan owners were offered a fully-serviced pitch which they can use all the year round and pay a monthly ground rent. The maximum continuous occupation permitted was three weeks. This has proved to be very popular.

Top photo shows the exit barriers. Bottom photo shows the road leading to the Health and Fitness Club. During the period 2008-14 Sam made many great improvements to this very attractive campsite and at the same time he retained its rural and natural features. Photos by JW, August 2014

Separately in 1989, a Health and Fitness Club with a special level deck 25-metre swimming pool was added. When this quite special development was completed, an open day was organized and the building was opened by Lord Shelburne (now the Marquis of Lansdowne, who kindly wrote the preface for this book), the owner of the famous Bowood Estate, which is close by. Initially this was intended for the campers. For various reasons this did not work out and it is now successfully run as a members-only club. The campsite is now one of the most pleasant in England and is attracting campers from around the world. I particularly enjoyed the development of Blackland Lakes and the business but the day to day running of it was not my scene.

Left: The 25-metre level deck pool. As a safety feature, the depth does not exceed one metre. In the top right hand photo, to the right of the flowers, is a children's pool. The yellow tube under the roof is part of the very efficient air-conditioning unit. Bottom left, the well-equipped gym and right, the exterior of the club

The advantage of a level deck pool is that the water is continually overflowing and returning to the main supply tank. It is easy to keep clean and more hygienic.

Postscript: On the 6th of August 2014, Sam was riding his powerful motorbike on a short break to visit a motor racing meeting in Belgium. Riding his motorbike was Sam's passion. He was nearly at his destination when he had a crash and was killed outright; he didn't suffer. This was an extremely sad and tragic end to a bright, kind, hardworking, brave and adventurous young man in the prime of life. He was 29 years old. During the time that Sam managed Blackland Lakes, and indeed the entire site, he made many improvements. JW is very proud of what he achieved. It was one of the loves of his life, probably the main one, next to motorbikes.

Following Sam's funeral, a well-attended barbecue was held in the evening at Blackland Lakes and the day was a celebration of Sam's life, which he led in the fast lane. (See Chapter 17, the Walden and Brunt families and special people.)

CHAPTER 13

BOATS AND BOATING, 1956-2009

Paddling kayaks, camping, learning to sail, big boat sailing

Some time after I had settled down to married life at Mead Cottage in Victoria Road, Trowbridge, I was introduced to canoeing by my middle brother Michael. Michael had recently bought a fairly beamy training canoe, built in Denmark by Jorgen Samson and named after the town where it was made, Struer. The construction used 7 skins of veneer. Both Michael and I had done quite a lot of canoeing in canvas-covered boats in our teens. We were now about 28 years old and Michael had spent a year at sea as an apprentice on an oil tanker, after which he did his two years' National Service driving tanks while I had spent a year in Canada driving Percheron horses.

By this time, Michael had mastered the stability of the craft and had taken the next step, which was to buy a K1 Attack, again built in Denmark by Jorgen Samson. It was an Olympic Class boat. I was able to borrow the training boat and in time I invested in a K1 model from the same builder. Whereas Michael's K1 was concave, mine was convex and slightly less stable. Paddling these boats was largely a question of balance and it took quite a while to become proficient. To begin with, numerous capsizes in cold water without a wetsuit were a regular feature. I always took a towel and a change of clothes in a waterproof bag.

Luckily Trowbridge was only a short distance from the Kennet and Avon Canal and the River Avon and this is where we practised. Canoeing is a great sport and is something one can do as an individual or with others. Michael and I joined Bradford on Avon Rowing Club (canoe section). Members of the club included Alex Moulton, who became famous for the invention of the rubber suspension for Mini cars and later for the small wheel Moulton bikes which he made in Bradford on Avon.

As Michael and I got fairly expert we regularly took part in canoe races which included Bath to Bradford, the Oxford canals and rivers and the river Exe from the beach at Dawlish Warren, in Devon. This one meant that you had to paddle along the Exeter Canal, passing quite large ships with about two feet to spare!

One of the races, which was perhaps the most exciting of them all, was the Poole Harbour race from Hamworthy Pier up the River Frome to Wareham. For this one, Michael and I had purchased a Struer Ribella K2. Originally the race was planned to go around Brownsea Island and then proceed up the river Frome. This particular day a force 5 wind was blowing and the course was shortened so that the canoes had to miss Brownsea and go round Green Island. The Harbour was quite choppy and part way around Green Island the K2 was filling with seawater. We were sinking! Fortunately we were both quite good swimmers and managed to swim ashore, pulling the submerged canoe with us. We tipped the water out and quickly re-joined the race. The person who presented the prizes was Blondie Haslar of 'Cockleshell Heroes' fame.

In my late twenties I was the proud father of two children, Hugh John (HJW) and Sarah-Jane. My wife Ann and I enjoyed the outdoors. For holidays we both preferred camping to Hotels or B&Bs. In fact I

JW paddling his K1 on the River Avon. Note collar and tie, I must have just finished work!

have never enjoyed staying in hotels, even very good ones. Horses for courses!

At the time I am referring to, between 1960 and 1965, it was possible to load up the car and take off to a spot 10, 50 or 100 miles away and ask a local farmer if we could put up our tent, possibly for a weekend or even for a two-week holiday. Nine times out of ten the farmer would make us welcome. Sometimes Michael and his family, two girls, Sally and Tessa, would come too and we had some super holidays. This is not normally possible today. (See www.gogreenadventurecamping.co.uk) Michael had a German Klepper family tent and mine was a Marachell, made in France. Both were very good by the current standards.

JW with his wife Ann, Hugh and Sarah enjoying the great outdoors

When Michael and I took up canoeing we often camped on the edge of Poole Harbour at Wytch Farm, owned by Farmer Tripp. Sometimes we were with our families, or, just with Members of Bradford on Avon Rowing Club. We enjoyed many super weekends and Bank Holidays and Poole Harbour is one of the best places in the UK for canoeing. In later years Mr Tripp's farm was taken over for drilling for oil and this continues today. Oil is now brought ashore from about two miles under the sea off Studland. From Wytch Farm it is sent by underground pipes to the refinery, probably at Fawley, on Southampton Water. Previously it was transported by road tankers.

Later I purchased a large second hand Volvo C150 4 x 4 which had been used by NATO forces and converted it into a camper. This served me well for a couple of years. It was petrol driven and quite thirsty. When it developed a serious radiator leak I sold it to a Duncan Gough, who was planning to use it to cross the Sahara Desert. He extended it by a metre by adding extra length in the middle. I'm not sure how the vehicle performed in the desert. Rather him than me!

For a brief period I had a 'Plastic' motor caravan which did not suit me as I preferred to go off road as much as possible. Very much later I 'invested' in an Austrian built 6 x 6 Pinzgauer. This came as a 'flatbed'. I engaged a body builder in Westbury (Spectra) to add a Body shell and then arranged for my eldest son Hugh to fit it out. Hugh, amongst other things, had attended the International Boat Building School at Lowestoft in Suffolk and was at this time building and repairing boats in Falmouth, Cornwall. He had become very skilled. The Pinzgauer was fitted out much like a boat with a sea going toilet, and none of the limited space was wasted. It accommodated a family of two adults and two young children in comfort. I made good use of the Pinzgauer, which was built like a tank. It is still in good working order after 20 years use. It never got stuck!

JW with the Pinzgauer at the Royal Show at Stoneleigh, Warwickshire, 1995.

In the snow at Heddington, near Calne, 2013

On one of our family camping holidays we headed for Fowey in Cornwall, in fact Polruan, on the eastern side of the River Fowey. Once we had set up camp I popped into the local pub to see if there was anyone who would teach me to sail in the two weeks I was staying there. I was lucky. I was introduced to a retired Royal Navy matelot who had his own 17ft deep-keeled Troy Class yacht. This fine fellow, whose name escapes me★, agreed to give me lessons daily from 10 am till noon. He was a good teacher. Fowey Harbour is quite tricky. There are dozens of moored boats all over the place. He quickly got me sailing and by the end of my holiday I was able to handle the boat pretty well. It was what you could call a crash course, but without any crashes!

★*I am indebted to Gerry Williams, a past Commodore of the Royal Fowey Yacht Club, who has advised me that the matelot was Walter Brennan, his father-in-law, and that Amethyst T5 was owned by a Mrs Hinder who lived in Polruan.*

During the two-week holiday we had two days of wet weather, very fine rain and the tent couldn't cope. Everything got wet through and we had to spend two nights in a B&B. The material used to make tents has made great strides since then and we would now have kept dry.

After this Cornish holiday I investigated the fairly wide range of boats which were available and selected a 14ft dinghy, the Kestrel. This was made of fiberglass by John Gmac in Fordingbridge, Hampshire. I contacted John and was offered a trial sail from Kehaven, near Lymington, to Yarmouth on the Isle of Wight, quite a voyage for a beginner. The boat performed well and I placed my order. I think John had made about 100 boats by that time. The class is still going strong and there are a number of them still racing at the Warsash Yacht Club on the River Hamble.

I soon took delivery, and to begin with I joined the Shearwater Sailing Club near Longleat. The 14 ft long Kestrel was somewhat too large for Shearwater which, while it was nearly a mile long, was in places quite narrow. Depending on the wind you were continually tacking. My good friend Tony King often sailed with me. Once we capsized and Tony was trapped under the boat. After, what seemed ages, Tony surfaced and all was well! I soon decided to join the Parkstone Yacht Club on the shores of Poole Harbour. This was much better and I had a lot of fun there. By this time I had reached the mature age of 30 and there would be a gap of some 20 years before I bought my next larger boat. During this time I devoted my leisure activities to horses (see Chapter 15). Tony concentrated on dinghy sailing and among many expeditions with Peter Barlow he sailed a 16ft Fireball, built by Peter, to the Scilly Isles.

Troy class yachts racing in Fowey Harbour   *The Kestrel dinghy*

I soon took delivery and to begin with I joined the Shearwater Sailing Club near Longleat. The 14 ft long Kestrel was somewhat too large for Shearwater, which, while it was nearly a mile long, was in places quite narrow. Depending on the wind you were continually tacking. My good friend Tony King often sailed with me. Once we capsized and Tony was trapped under the boat. After, what seemed ages, he surfaced and all was well!

I soon decided to join the Parkstone Yacht Club on the shores of Poole Harbour. This was much better and I had a lot of fun there. By this time I had reached the mature age of 30 and there would be a gap of some 20 years before I bought a larger boat. During this time I devoted my leisure activities to horses (see Chapter 15, "In the Saddle, Horses and Hunting").

While I was without a boat of my own I was fortunate enough to accompany my brother Michael on his wooden yacht, a Hillyard called *Trimley Maid*. Earlier I had taught Michael to sail and he was now very experienced. On one particular sail to Alderney in the Channel Islands we left Braye Harbour in patchy fog bound for Poole, which is about 60 miles away.

All boats crossing the English Channel have to negotiate two shipping lanes which are five miles apart. In the nearest one to Alderney the ships travel from west to east and the next one east to west. Most of the ships are about half a mile apart, one behind the other, although the faster ones will overtake the slower ones. All vessels crossing the very busy shipping lanes must give priority to big ships and always, when close, go around the stern.

On this occasion we knew we were close to the westward bound shipping, but suddenly a blanket of fog descended on *Trimley Maid* and visibility dropped to about 70 yards. Out of the fog a massive cargo vessel appeared, heading straight for us. Michael was on the helm and as quick as a flash, he swung the boat through 90 degrees. We had a very near miss!

Trimley Maid was not equipped with radar at that time. There was no sign of a lookout on board. They were probably all asleep! The ship was Russian, returning from Cuba. It was at the time of the Cuban missile crisis, which was only resolved by the determined action of President John F Kennedy.

Trimley Maid, *brother Michael's pride and joy. He sailed her thousands of miles over a 30-year period.*

On several other occasions I was fortunate to sail with Noel Knee, the boss of Knees Group in Trowbridge. Noel had a Harrison Butler designed wooden yacht named Greengage, which was moored in Poole Harbour. On one passage, returning from the Isle of Wight, we had a large spinnaker up and as we approached the Needles on the western side of the Island, by Alum Bay, the wind strengthened to the point where we had to get the sail down with the utmost urgency to avoid a disaster. Unfortunately the sail was jammed. We were being blown rapidly towards the shore completely out of control. With considerable effort, Noel was able to cut the sail loose and save Greengage and the three of us on board, the third one being Tony King.

On another passage, with Noel and Tony, we crossed the English Channel from Poole to Cherbourg, a distance of about 60 miles. At an average speed of 5 knots this would take about 12 hours. The crossing was uneventful until we were about five miles off the French coast, when we ran into thick fog. In those days we didn't have the luxury of a GPS, only a depth sounder. At this point of the trip I was on the helm and suddenly, out of the fog most of the French fleet of warships were bearing down on us. I had to alter course, and this put out our reckoning completely. One way to find our position was by the depth of water below the hull of the boat. The continental shelf starts a few miles from the French coast and as all navigation charts show the depth of water, particularly near land, we were able to use the depth sounder and establish our position. We were about five miles from the coast, so we pressed on to Cherbourg, where we had a very pleasant time.

A passage from Plymouth to St Malo on the tall ship *Malcolm Millar*

Around 1986 I had the opportunity to join a Tall Ship, the *Malcolm Miller*, which was due to sail from Plymouth to St Malo in Brittany. My brother Michael had been offered three berths on the ship. I took one and the other was taken by a mutual friend, Geoff Stone.

At that time I was driving a large rather cumbersome Mercedes and the three of us set out for Plymouth which is about 160 miles from Trowbridge. We boarded the ship at Plymouth Hoe, where Drake had been playing bowls when he was told the Spanish Amada had been sighted off the Devon coast. He finished his game before preparing for

battle. We didn't expect to have a battle with Spain, but we had one with the wind and the sea!

The Malcolm Millar

We put to sea around noon, the day after we arrived, and headed out into the English Channel, which the French, just to be awkward, call La Manche, which translated into English, is The Sleeve! The weather was unsettled and progressively the sea got quite rough. There was a paid crew of about six. The remainder were volunteers who had paid a nominal sum for the privilege of a voyage on a tall ship. Before putting to sea we had been shown the ropes and split into watches, about 10 in each group. I was placed in the mizzen watch which is at the rear (the stern) of the ship, where the mizzen mast and mizzen sail are situated. There were two other watches to cover 24 hours, the main watch, in the middle (amidships) of the ship and the fore watch in the front, or bow. Each watch did a 4-hour stint on duty and four hours off, in other words two 4 hour watches in 24 hours.

My last watch on the first day at sea ended at midnight. When you were on watch your main duties were to attend to the sails, and when I came on deck at 0400 hours it was complete chaos. Exactly at that moment the mizzen sail split completely from side to side about 3 feet from the bottom. The wind was force 10 and there was no sign of the skipper. When he appeared he looked as though he had had a rough night! I certainly had, I was a sick as a dog!

Before he had turned in the night before he had, correctly, decided to remain in the Channel overnight rather than risking closing on Alderney and the dangerous seas around the Channel Islands.

For another 3 hours we cruised up and down the Channel until the storm abated and then headed for St Malo. We were at least 12 hours behind schedule and had little time to enjoy St Malo, which is quite special. We were directed into the Inner Dock, where the ship was dressed overall, and the able-bodied among the crew were sent up into the rigging. I don't have a head for heights and stayed on deck. Michael, on the other hand, who was often at the top of the highest tree he could find, went right to the top of the main mast.

The visit to St Malo was far too short and it would have been well worth spending several days there. We put to sea the following morning and headed for Plymouth. This sail was uneventful and enjoyable and definitely made up for the outward passage.

The three of us, and especially me, had had very little sleep. I had been very seasick during the storm and had barely recovered when i went on watch at the height of the storm. I wasn't really in a fit state to drive, but there wasn't any choice. We all had to get back to work.

We pressed on regardless and as we approached Taunton Deane Services there were some road works where the road was cordoned off with numerous cones. I fell asleep at this critical point and drove right along the row of cones, flattening most of them. It was a rude awakening! Fortunately, no one was hurt and the car had only some minor scratches. We pulled into the service area, had several cups of strong coffee to revive and got home safely in time for supper. I have never been seasick since!

A cruise around the Western Isles of Scotland

About 1989 I was introduced to a retired bank manager, Sam Crabb, and asked him if he fancied a sailing holiday. He hadn't sailed before, but he was willing to give it a try. I had been looking in a yachting magazine and had spotted a sailing holiday on a ketch around the Western Isles. I duly booked it and we set off in my Mercedes once again.

The journey to Oban was about 450 miles. By the time we had done about 400 we had had enough. We found a comfortable B&B and completed the final 50 miles next morning and reported to the boat. The skipper was on deck and told us, in a rather offhand way, to buzz off and come back at the correct time for going aboard. This wasn't the kind of welcome we were expecting, but reluctantly we did as we were told.

Luckily, things improved afterwards. The Ketch was called the

Corryvreckan, named after a very dangerous whirlpool between the islands of Jura and Scarba. She was well found, about 40 feet long and carried a crew of three plus 12 paying passengers who were expected to help sail the boat .This suited me and I was able to take a turn on the helm. The skipper's wife was a Cordon Bleu cook and one of the best features of the holiday was the excellent 'cuisine'!

We set off next morning bound for the Isle of Mull about 10 miles away. Here we dropped anchor and went ashore for a brief look round. Back to sea next morning we were accompanied by several dolphins and also spotted a large sea eagle on a nearby cliff. My memory of the early part of this trip is somewhat obscure. We did visit several islands and the scenery is beautiful. We also passed close to the Corryvreckan whirlpool. I am not quite sure whether we had value for money, as the skipper had planned to shorten the cruise so that he could take the boat to near the Firth of Clyde for a winter refit. As this meant that we would be going through the Crinan Canal, this probably made up for it. To begin with it was very wet when we entered the canal and we had a lot of locks to open and close. By the time we reached the other end the sun was shining and as we entered Loch Fyne and headed for the Firth of Clyde we were joined by a Royal Navy nuclear submarine. This was returning to its base at Faslane, following a three-month tour of duty under the sea. It was very impressive.

Using the canal shortens the journey to the Clyde by some 140 miles. The boatyard chosen for the refit covered at least three acres. During WW2 it was used to build air sea rescue launches, which saved hundreds of air crew who had been shot down. I am pleased to have been through the Crinan Canal and also to have visited many of the Western Isles.

In 1984, after 20 years with horses, I decided to take up sailing again. This time I considered something larger than the Kestrel. I had read about a design called a Vertue. This would be very good but a little

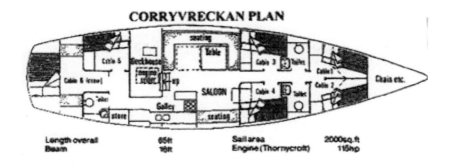

Plan of the ketch Corryvreckan. *Ideal for a family charter holiday.*

cramped, as I now had a young family. The Vertue was designed for single-handed sailing and had made many transatlantic crossings. I believe one was raced by Blondie Hasler, the Cockleshell Hero. I found that the same designer, Laurent Giles, had designed a slightly larger version called a Normandy. I scanned the adverts in the yachting press and found one based at Lymington. This one was called *Gilliflower*, named after a South African flower.

I had her surveyed, which established that a lot of work needed to be done. A sensible price was agreed and I had her moved by road to Knights Marsh Farm. My eldest son Hugh, who was at that time building wooden boats, advised me how to restore *Gilliflower* and I set about it with all speed. It was a major task, but I managed it successfully. *Gilliflower* was restored to her former glory in about six months, and I had her taken to Poole Harbour, where I had booked a swinging mooring from Harry Price at Hamworthy. Having a deep keeled boat is quite different to a dinghy, and Poole Harbour has plenty of shallow areas and odd sandbanks which are exposed at low tide. It is essential to keep within the marked channels, some of which are very narrow, only a matter of a few feet.

It took me quite a while to get used to my new toy and once or

twice i was aground on a sandbank with the tide going out at great speed. This means that you have to wait for several hours before you are re-floated and during that time the boat lies on its side, which is most uncomfortable, to say the least! You can imagine what the 'missus' thought, especially if it was time to feed a hungry crew! I was in the doghouse, with threats such as 'That's the last time I'm coming sailing with you!'

During the winter while I was working on *Gilliflower*, I attended a navigation course at Chippenham College. Anyone

Gilliflower on passage from Brittany to Poole, 1986

who owns a seagoing vessel should be sure to take one of these courses, which are run under the auspices of the Royal Yachting Association (RYA). They give you the essential basics of navigation - without this knowledge you would soon be in trouble. The course incorporates the use of a marine ship to shore and shore to ship radio. Before embarking on a passage, lots of local sailing is essential. If you can navigate Poole Harbour, that is a good start. Getting used to the tides is absolutely vital. It is much more dangerous when you are sailing near to land than when you are well away from it!

My first seagoing passage with *Gilliflower*

Towards the end of my first summer with *Gilliflower* my brother Michael, who owned *Trimley Maid*, persuaded me to sail *Gilliflower* to the Channel Islands and Brittany. The plan was that we would sail the two boats together. As I had not planned a passage at this stage I relied on Michael to do this and to navigate as well (actually it is quite easy from Poole as Alderney is practically due south!) We set off at the unearthly hour of 1 am to take advantage of the tide going out of Poole Harbour. It was pitch black and to follow the channel when you leave the harbour with no lights it is quite difficult. We just managed to see the channel buoys and one we nearly hit as it only came in view when we were a couple of yards from it.

Old Harry Rocks - a welcome landmark when homeward bound to Poole

Once we cleared Old Harry Rocks off Studland, we were in the open sea and made good progress with a steady south westerly breeze. It is lovely to sail without the noise and vibration of an engine. To begin with we were sailing with *Trimley Maid* in sight. At about four in the morning the sun began to rise and so did the morale of the crew. Only one slight problem, where was *Trimley Maid*? We pressed on and didn't see her again until next day. The 'expert', Michael, had got his knickers in a twist and ended up on the east side of the Cherbourg peninsula. I think the excuse was that he had been seasick. My amateur navigation skills were spot on, and having passed through both the west and east bound shipping lanes we had Alderney in sight. Land ahoy! We had also got the tides right for passing through the Alderney Race, which runs at about 17 knots between Alderney and the Cherbourg peninsula. If you get that wrong you will be going backwards!

We put into Beaucette Marina on the north east corner of Guernsey. This marina, which was originally made and used by the military, had literally been blown out of the rocks with high explosive. It was necessary to enter this marina at high tide to clear a bar at the entrance. Eventually Michael arrived and put into St Peter Port Marina, where we joined him next morning.

We spent just one night in St Peter Port Marina and set off early next morning for Lezardrieux in Brittany, which would be about 35 miles away. Lezardrieux lies some way up an estuary and we arrived in the estuary about teatime. Michael, the senior navigator, selected a spot to anchor, having allowed for the fall of the tide, so he thought. Unfortunately at 11 pm that night the tide was rapidly going out. We had to 'up anchor' and move into deeper water sharpish!

Next morning, before sailing up the estuary to the small town, we went ashore to find a good *Boucherie*. I bought some French sausages and they were some of the best I have ever had. Later that day Michael, who had been to Lezardrieux before, hired a taxi. He took us to a restaurant some five miles inland, where he introduced us to some French cuisine, especially escargots (snails) which were very good.

As time was limited, work was calling; we headed for home calling at Braye, the main Harbour on the North coast of Alderney. This island is one of my favourites and I have been there many times since. *Gilliflower*, which displaced about 4 tons, was more of a racing Boat than *Trimley Maid,* which displaced 9 tons. On the passage from Lezardrieux we frequently had to wait for *Trimley Maid* or there was a risk of losing sight of her a second time. *Trimley Maid* is by far the better vessel for cruising and Michael enjoyed many long distance cruises in her, including the Caribbean. The evening we left Braye Harbour, the weather turned foul. About five miles out, visibility in the darkness, was nil. We found ourselves surrounded by French fishing boats, and we could hear them but not see them. I hoped they had radar and could see us.

We pressed on, and with the early dawn we saw Blighty again. 'Land Ahoy!' shouts the first crew member to spot Portland Bill. We raised more sail and were soon back in Poole in time for a good breakfast.

My crews on that trip were Julian Carpenter and Ralph Scott. At one stage of the outgoing passage both of them were violently seasick and were laid low. Fortunately they had recovered when we were homeward bound from Alderney.

I kept *Gilliflower* for about five years and had a lot of fun with her, mainly in and round Poole Harbour and the south coast. But she was not designed for cruising, and I decided to look for something more suitable.

Julian Carpenter.
When he sailed with
me he would have
been about 21.

Gilliflower with Michael Carpenter (Julian's older brother), JW in cap

An exciting passage from Falmouth to Poole

Sometime around 1995 my boatbuilding son, Hugh, was building and repairing boats in the Falmouth area and one he was working on was a 34ft Bermudan-rigged yacht called *Susanna*.

Susanna was a Dalimore design and the owner, Alfred Able, happened to live near me at Calne. Hugh was taken with this boat and persuaded me to organize a trial sail with a view to possibly buying her. This I did. I took my brother Michael, together with Alfie Able, to Falmouth and we had a sail to Fowey, where we tied up for the night. Michael and I were very impressed and I told Alfred that I would consider making him an offer. Before doing so, I suggested to Alfie, who had retired from sailing, that *Susanna* should be brought back to Poole, which would be more convenient for him and me. Alfie agreed and I set to work to organize a crew. What began as a reasonable proposition turned out to be quite eventful but, fortunately, not a disaster!

Susanna

I found a crew of three. One was Ralph Scott, who had sailed with me on *Gilliflower,* and the other two were young Royal Navy submariners. The four of us loaded up my Daihatsu Fourtrack and headed for Falmouth. *Susanna* had been neglected for some time and needed a good airing to freshen her up and clear the dampness. We stowed everything for the passage and planned to sail next day with the tide. The initial plan was that providing the engine was running satisfactorily and we had cleared Falmouth Harbour, we would head for Salcombe under sail. I calculated that by leaving around midday we would reach Salcombe at high tide, about 2300 hours, when it would be possible to cross the bar at the Harbour entrance. So far so good!

Susanna is a very well designed and seaworthy yacht and we had a super sail to Salcombe, passing quite close to the Eddystone Lighthouse, about four miles off Plymouth. The Wind was a south westerly between force 4 and 5, just right, and we made a steady 7 knots. As planned we were abreast of Salcombe just before 2300 hrs. The tide allowed us to clear the bar and with the sails taken down we entered the Harbour using the engine.

I mentioned that *Susanna* had been neglected for a considerable time. Unknown to me it must have been a year or more. When diesel is left in a tank for extended periods, or the tank had never been cleaned out, a certain amount of sludge builds up and this can cause a blockage in the fuel system. Guess what, we had a blockage!

No sooner had we cleared the bar than the engine stopped and we were adrift. It was pitch black. To try and keep some control I got the crew to raise the jib, and with this and a good torch we able to find a buoy to which we made fast. There was nothing more we could do at that time of night, so we turned in for some much-needed sleep. Being responsible for both the boat and crew is quite demanding. My young submariners had had little experience under sail, more underwater!

At first light, I set about stripping the fuel system down, cleaning the fuel filters and then reassembling it all. The Harbourmaster appeared alongside and requested that we moved off his buoy. Luckily I got the engine going and we made our way towards Salcombe Quay. Part way the engine failed again. This was because I hadn't cleaned out the tank. Ralph Scott volunteered to go ashore and try and find a marine engineer and some clean diesel. He came back with both, while in the meantime I stripped the system down a second time. To avoid the gunge getting into the engine again I got the engineer to connect the clean fuel direct to the engine. This was done and we soon motored out of the Harbour, heading for Weymouth.

My plan was that we would put into Weymouth for at least one night. However one of the submariners was extremely anxious to get back to Poole, where he had a girlfriend. As one always does before embarking on a passage, i had studied the weather forecast and had established that there was a good slot in the weather to sail direct to Poole. I listened to the shipping forecast very carefully and concluded that providing we were in Poole by 0100 hours, we would avoid a storm which was expected about 0300 hours. I agreed to head direct for Poole.

Susanna had a very high mast, in fact excessively high, and I understand that a previous owner had had it extended. This meant that she could carry too much sail. In the conditions in which we left Salcombe this was fine, and we had a super sail across Lyme Bay and on towards Swanage.

It is normal that the crew rotate their watch duty. Depending on the length of the passage, the skipper would have a 'kip' when he is satisfied that all is well. Before we left Salcombe, one of my crew, Ralph Scott, who had been violently sick on the passage from Falmouth to Salcombe (and on a previous passage on *Gilliflower*), 'jumped ship' and went home by bus! This meant that I was only able to let my remaining crew have a two-hour rest each and then, leaving them on watch together, I would take a turn below.

I had just got settled at about 2300 hours when one of them shouted down the hatch, 'Come quick, we are in trouble'. We certainly were! I scrambled back into my heavy weather kit and peered out of the hatch. It was utterly pitch black; not a light to be seen. The rain was practically solid and was crossing the boat horizontally. The forecasters had got it wrong that night, rather like in 1987 when the TV forecaster Michael Fish had said 'Don't worry, there won't be a hurricane' and of course there was. A real howler!

The wind was blowing in excess of force 9 and gusting up to 11. I had previously experienced Force 9, but nothing like this. I knew that we were somewhere off Swanage and luckily the wind was taking us away from the rocky shore. Practically the only good thing I can say about my crew, apart from the fact that they were both decent chaps, is that neither of them panicked. What they should have done before the wind got too strong was to get the massive main sail down. With a big effort we managed to get it down as quick as we could and all the others as well. I then started the engine and set course for Poole, which would have been about five miles off. Very shortly we rounded the headland off Swanage, which links up with Old Harry Rocks at Studland, and by then the storm had eased very slightly and visibility had improved. We could just pick out Bournemouth lights. Wind always blows much stronger close to a headland.

We were safe, but our troubles were far from over. None of us are ever too old to learn, and I learned something that night which is worth passing on. Marine diesels are designed so that the fuel from the tank, when it arrives at the engine, is in excess of what the engine requires. The surplus passes back to the tank. The marine engineer should have been aware of this when he connected the five gallons to the engine and charged me £80 for doing so! All the surplus fuel was returning to the main tank and mixing with the sludge. In about half an hour the clean fuel was either used or returned and the engine packed up once again. What he should have done was to make sure the surplus fuel was returned to the clean secondary tank which he had brought on board.

We dropped the anchor and I then had to decide the best course of action. It was still blowing force 8 to 9 and raining hard. I called the coastguard and explained the situation, which was that we were safe but uncomfortable and would be OK until the morning. By now it was about 0200 hours and still very wet and windy. The coastguard very quickly said they would send out the Poole lifeboat and give us a tow into Poole. This is what I had hoped for, and in about half an hour they were alongside. One of the lifeboat crew jumped on to Susanna with a line which he made fast. Next, we tried to bring up the anchor. It was jammed solid on some obstruction on the bottom, most likely a wreck. The best thing to have done would have been to put a buoy on the end of the chain before cutting it, but the lifeboat crew was in too much of a rush to do this and promptly cut the chain, which went to the bottom with the anchor, about £400 pounds worth!.

We were soon tied up safely alongside Poole Quay, where the

lifeboat had left us. It was about 5 am, and we turned in for a couple of hours' sleep. At 8 am, once again, I stripped the fuel system down. By now I could nearly do it with my eyes shut, and one of my crew fetched some diesel. Until this point I wasn't aware of the system I explained earlier. I decided to go through the Poole Lifting Bridge into Holes Bay, where I knew I could find a mooring. As before the engine started, and I assumed we had put in sufficient fuel to reach the mooring. I was wrong. This time we had moved much less than a mile from the bridge when it snuffed it again. We were adrift, 'up the creek without a paddle', and no brakes!

All I could do was to steer towards the lifeboat, which was tied up on the lifeboat quay. we managed to get a line on to the lifeboat and made fast. Luckily the lifeboat staff were very understanding and helped me sort things out. They explained about the fuel system, and with their advice we arranged that the surplus fuel was returned to the secondary tank. With this done we made our way to the mooring in Holes Bay, then went ashore and made our way by road back to Calne.

The moral of this is never go to sea with a rank full of sludge and if you do, couple a secondary tank so that the surplus fuel is not mixed with the rubbish. It was a lesson hard learnt, but the sailing was great and made up for it. I didn't buy *Susanna* and Alfie Able insisted that I replaced the anchor and chain and had the jib, which had slit from one side to the other, repaired. I have seen *Susanna* once since in the Solent and she had been restored to her former glory. A lovely boat! The expensive so-called marine engineer in Salcombe should have been sent a massive bill and been retrained or sacked. Sometime later I was in Poole Yacht Club with Brother Michael and related my tale to the club steward. He remembered that particular night. He lived in a flat above the club and stored his dustbins on the flat roof. The wind had blown them off the roof and the clatter had rudely awakened him!

Sparky, a steel gaff-rigged Wylo II

In 1989 I was searching for a yacht which would fulfil my desire to go to sea in any weather and at the same time be able to accommodate my family in reasonable comfort. My view, at that time, of glass fibre/plastic vessels was somewhat negative. Many of them were like large plastic bath tubs. Additionally, the problem with osmosis had not yet been overcome. I began to consider steel. One of the books I had read was 'Voyaging on a Low Income' by Annie Hill, and a chapter in Annie's book described a steel yacht designed by Nick Skeates. The more I studied them the more I was convinced that this would suit me down to the ground or, more to the point, the last nut and bolt!

Luckily, Annie's book included enough information to enable me to contact Nick through his mother, Nick being in the Pacific on the original Wylo II at that time. Mrs Skeates said she would put me in touch with him when she next heard from him. When a couple of weeks went by with no news, I gave Mrs Skeates another ring and she suggested that

Sparky arrives from Essex at Davis's boatyard in Poole Harbour, 1989

I contact John Strut, who had built a Wylo II. This I did and I arranged to meet him in Essex. John, apart from being an experienced sailor, was a very skilled engineer and had built the boat, which he named *Sparky*, in his garden some five years previously. *Sparky* was now out of the water at a boatyard. John explained all the intricacies of a quite special boat of which he was justly proud. As she was practically new and in pristine condition, an expensive survey was avoided.

Tony Russell with Bernie and Mike at the Ploumanac'h Festival

JW and the two policemen who sailed with me

Sparky racing in the Solent with the OGA, JW standing, his son Sam on the helm

Sam and Maggie Baylis

Brilleau *at anchor in the Caribbean*

Nick Skeates originally had a wooden yacht called Wylo, but while on a circumnavigation of the world and sailing around the Great Barrier Reef some 30 years ago, he hit a reef and sank. The story goes that he was down below with his lady companion and giving her more attention than the sailing! Luckily they were both saved and Nick, without a boat, stayed in New Zealand for sufficient time to design and build a replacement. The result was the Wylo II, and Nick has been living on this for over 30 years. During this time Nick has been selling Plans of Wylo II and, in a number of cases, has helped build them. The design is ideal for self-building and there are now well over 40 Wylo II boats spread around the world, mainly in New Zealand, South Africa and the UK. Should you require more information visit Nick's website?

John Strut was persuaded to part with *Sparky* at a realistic figure. Luckily there was a fellow in the boatyard repairing his boat trailer. I asked if he could take *Sparky* to Poole and what he would charge. He thought for a moment. He had just been booked to bring a boat from Plymouth to Essex and would take *Sparky* to Poole on the way. For what could have cost around £400 (worth £1000 in 2013) I agreed to pay £200.

I had *Sparky* delivered to Davis's boatyard in Holes Bay, Poole. One of the advantages of the Wylo II is that two people can raise and lower the mast from its tabernacle with the aid of the hinged A frame fitted to the bow, ideal if you decided to go through French canals. Once *Sparky* was rigged, including the fitting of Simpson davits to carry my Tinker dinghy, I moved her with my crew, Julian Carpenter, to one of Harry Price's moorings near Hamworthy Pier. Harry Price managed probably 70 or so moorings in the harbour. He was well equipped with a powerful work boat, fitted with a crane for lifting his moorings. Harry became a good friend and I was glad of his help on a number of occasions.

Sparky alongside. A fine, safe and seaworthy vessel, ideal for self-building. Note the mast stepped in a tabernacle, which, using the A Frame enables the mast to be lowered for negotiating low bridges. Essential for the French canals.

Nick Skeates, exceptional ocean sailor, designer of the Wylo II and good friend

Sparky, when compared with many other yachts, had numerous special features in addition to the unique A frame. She was extremely seaworthy and tough. The deck was the full width of the vessel (10 ft), which was a great advantage for working on deck handling the many sails, as well as sunbathing! The fact that she was gaff rigged meant that the sails were both much easier to handle and far more flexible than a Bermudan-rigged boat such as *Susanna*. She also had a self-setting stay sail. When going about, the only sail requiring attention was the jib. She was designed for single-handed sailing.

The speed of a sailing boat is largely determined by the length of the hull at the waterline – the longer the ship, the faster she goes. Seven knots was *Sparky's* optimum speed unless you had the help of the tide. There were a number of versions of Wylo IIs. *Sparky* had a two-tonne solid keel running the length of the vessel, plus a lifting keel. This gives a draft of one metre with the keel up and two metres with it down, ideal for navigating rivers and creeks. Any water in the bilge is pumped out through the keel housing and to lower and raise the keel is done by a rope conveniently made fast in the cockpit.

Sparky was spacious down below, with full headroom. She had two cabins and depending on the makeup of the crew, can accommodate 6 adults, one in a single berth, four in two double bunks and one in a pilot berth. I have had eight on board with two camping on the deck! She has two Taylor paraffin stoves, one for cooking and one for heating, which I found to be very good once I got the measure of them.

As I spent quite a lot of time on board in the winter I got my very good friend Ernie Hiscock, of Hiscock engineers in Trowbridge, to make and install a wood-burning stove, which was a good move. I had to take care with it, however - once or twice I had it literally red hot! One thing which *Sparky* lacked was adequate insulation. On one night I spent alongside at Ridge Wharf, the outside temperature registered - 10 C and the River Frome froze over. I nearly did too!

As I wrote this chapter, very tragic news had just come through concerning the yacht *Cheeki Rafiki*, from which four sailors were lost in May 2014. More than a week later the boat was finally found upturned, without its keel. I was not surprised to hear this, as the keel of a yacht is very vulnerable. It was obvious that it had failed somehow and the ship had capsized without warning.

I was pleased that I chose the Steel Wylo II. Leaving Braye Harbour one morning I hit a submerged rock. As *Sparky* was well built of steel with a solid two-tonne keel plus a lifting keel, the only damage was that the rudder was knocked off the lower Pintle. I was still able to maintain steerage. Subsequently, I was told that the damage to *Cheeki Rafiki* most likely occurred before she put to sea. A very rough sea could have knocked it off. Food for thought!

Two cruises on *Sparky*

My first seagoing venture on *Sparky* was to the Maritime Festival at Ploumanac'h in Brittany. It was about five years since I had sold

Gilliflower so I was fortunate to have as my crew two policemen, Mike and Bernie who had had considerably more sailing experience than me. There was a slight setback before we set sail from Poole. One of the crew mistakenly dropped the anchor, which got tangled up with the mooring. When these two strong fellows tried to force it up they ruined the windlass, which meant a costly replacement. Rather than delay our departure, we let the anchor go. I left a message with Harry Price and when we returned, Harry had rescued the anchor and chain. Fortunately I had a spare one, which is always a good thing, but not a windlass.

The Channel crossing must have been uneventful, as I have no memory of it. We put into St Peter Port, Guernsey, on the way and the remainder of the passage was through poor visibility. We did have sight of the Roches Douvres, which is a good landmark. The Harbour at Ploumanac'h is set back some distance from the sea and is entered through a narrow channel between high cliffs and a lot of rocks. Once inside we were able to go alongside a pontoon, from which we launched the tinker dinghy to go ashore. This festival is always well attended and there were several other British boats there including that of some friends of mine, Sam and Maggie Baylis, another Wylo II, *Brilleau*. We thoroughly enjoyed ourselves with plenty of good food, music and dancing. Policemen off duty often let their hair down and consume more beer than is good for them. At least my crew did and one ended up dancing on the tables. The friendly Frenchmen took it all in good heart!

When you undertake your first fairly long passage it is definitely wise to have at least one crew member who is experienced. I was pleased I had one on this trip. On the homeward passage we anchored in a small bay on the southernmost tip of Guernsey. It was a very deep anchorage and the anchor chain only just touched the seabed. Next day we headed for Poole. By dusk we were close to the westbound shipping lane, which was very busy. The visibility was good and we were able to see all the navigation lights (green on the starboard side showing that the boats were moving to the right) so that we were able to pass safely between the ships, which travel at over 20 knots. We had a good crossing to Poole.

On another occasion, Mike sailed with me to Weymouth. On the way we put into Lulworth Cove and spent the evening in the local pub. My crew, as before, drank far too much, (more than eight pints!) Next morning at about 0600 hours, I noticed that we were drifting towards the shore – not enough chain let out the night before. I was unable to get any sense out of my crew but I managed to get the sails up and put to sea myself. We ran straight into a violent thunderstorm, and still my crew didn't appear. The Lulworth military firing range is either side and behind the cove, and as there was to be some firing that morning their safety launch came close and instructed me to move away as quickly as possible.

I haven't asked either policeman to sail with me again. However, both were sound fellows and I am sure were very good policemen.

The Old Gaffers' Association

Shortly after I bought *Sparky* I made contact with the Solent area of the OGA and particularly Sam and Maggie Baylis. Normally I am not a very clubby person, preferring to be independent. There were two exceptions; the OGA was one and the Bradford on Avon Rowing Club the other. I joined the OGA and the next 15 years were some of the best I have had, comparable to my many years with horses.

Sparky was still based in Poole and I had moved her to a cheaper mooring on the River Frome at Ridge. To get to the Solent to take part in the OGA events, mainly racing, this meant a minimum of two days' absence from my home, which was 60 odd miles away. There were two other OGA members with boats in Poole Harbour; Mark Woodhouse with *Foxhound* and Mike and Dan Shaw with *Susan J*. Frequently, we would make the return crossing from the Solent at the same time. *Foxhound* was always the quickest, and then *Susan J* followed by *Sparky*, which was designed for ocean cruising rather than racing. On one crossing in very rough weather, after we had cleared the Needles on the western end of the Isle of Wight, we lost sight of *Susan J*. Whereas *Sparky* had a self-draining cockpit, *Susan J* didn't. Apparently she took on a lot of water and had to be bailed out. While doing so the tide and wind took them to the south east of the Needles. Eventually they caught us up. I remember that on the same crossing a force 7-8 onshore wind was taking us too close for comfort to Bournemouth Pier and shallow water. I had to start the engine with some urgency. We all got safely into Poole.

My wife Barbara, together with my younger son Joseph, then about eight years old, had sailed with me to the Solent the previous day. As we entered the Solent via the Needles passage the sea was extremely rough. Barbara declined to sail with me back to Poole and I don't think she sailed with me again! She took the train home with Joseph. My older son, Sam, and one of his friends sailed back with m\e. Sam was already a competent sailor and accompanied me on most of my trips to the Solent and further afield. In due course Joseph came too, and we had some super sailing.

In time I was asked to be the OGA representative for Poole, which I was happy to accept. I organized several events there: a race in Bournemouth Bay with the help of Mark Woodhouse, one or two BBQs at Goathorn in Poole Harbour, an evening at Mark's brewery at Blandford and a BBQ on one of the Poole passenger boats. After a while I decided I would try and find a mooring in the Solent to cut down the time spent in getting to and from the Solent, which, with the journey from Calne, was a day each way.

Mark Pooke - great friend, super crew and an accomplished artist

Dave Randall and the new President (2012), Dan Shaw, of the Solent OGA, at a BBQ

An OGA barbecue at Goat Horn in Poole Harbour, organized by JW

I found that there were about 5 Wylo II class boats in and around the Solent and these were being added to each year. I got to know the owners, who were all members of the OGA. John Richardson and his wife Wendy had built a 35ft version named *Island Swift* (IS). With its extended hull length and larger sails, IS was considerably faster than *Sparky*. Others were Sam and Maggie Baylis with *Brilleau*, Martin Morris with *Apple* and Graeme Hawksley, who was building one designed to be powered by electricity generated by the movement of the boat through the water.

Sam and Maggie Baylis racing Brilleau *with the OGA*

John and Wendy Richardson, great sailors and great friends, on board Sparky

John Richardson's brother Tom ran the Elephant Boatyard at Burlesdon on the River Hamble, which is about two miles upriver from Southampton Water. Through John, I was able to get a berth for *Sparky* at the boatyard which was very convenient and time saving. The Elephant Boatyard has been established for very many years. The very successful TV series 'Howard's Way' was filmed there. Tom, his manager Brian Crawley and the staff were always very helpful. They looked after *Sparky* and on some occasions, me as well, which I always appreciated. I berthed *Sparky* there for getting on for 10 years.

Coinciding with moving *Sparky* to the River Hamble, I moved to Bishops Waltham, which, as by this time I had retired from business, gave me the opportunity to sail more often. Initially I was short of a crew. I placed a card in the local Post Office window and had one reply, from Mark Pooke, a very skilled engineering draughtsman whose main task at that time was designing escape mechanisms for submarines worldwide. He is also a brilliant artist, specializing in seascapes and Boats. One afternoon *Sparky* was practically out of fuel. Mark and I decided to motor her down river about a mile to the floating fuel station. Mark was holding the mooring line ready to cast off and jump on board while I started the engine. It ran for about 30 seconds and stopped, out of fuel.

The tide was ebbing rapidly and it was more than Mark could do to hold on to *Sparky*. To avoid a cold ducking he let go, and I was adrift. Really up the creek without a paddle! Luckily I was able to steer but had no brakes. There were dozens of boats returning to their berths from a day's sailing. I made a lot of gestures to the oncoming boats and luckily one skipper got the message. He came alongside, threw me a line and then pushed me to the nearest free pontoon, where with considerable effort, fighting the strong ebbing tide, I was able to make fast. There are thousands of boats on the River Hamble and very few free berths. Enough excitement for one day!

Later I got to know Rene Brent, a skilled sailmaker who concentrated on boat covers, and his son Eduardo. Eduardo often sailed with me. He is a super crew and jolly good company. On one trip to Poole with a nice lady for company, Kay Harris, we anchored close to, or just in, a minor channel close to Brownsea Island. The chart and my depth sounder showed adequate depth, even at low tide, so we launched the dinghy from the davits and spent a couple of hours wandering around Brownsea. When we had completed our tour and looked out over the Harbour to where *Sparky* was anchored, we were dismayed to see that she was high and dry with about 4 feet from the deck to the mud below her. Either side was deep water. Boats were passing on each side of her!

My doctor in Bishops Waltham, Paul Hemming, and his colleague, David Ibbitson, came with me on numerous occasions. David owned a Kestrel dinghy which they both raced at Warsash sailing Club.

Sailing doctors Paul Hemming and David Ibbotson from Bishops Waltham

At the time I joined the OGA, Geoff Skinner was the Secretary and George Beckett the President. Many races were organized in the Solent. I hadn't had any racing experience when I joined, but as time went by I became quite proficient. *Sparky* performed much better when there was plenty of wind. One summer, John Richardson and his wife Wendy sailed *Island Swift* (IS) to the Mediterranean through the French canals and left their boat there for a couple of seasons. When John and Wendy were at home on the Isle of Wight without IS they frequently sailed with me on *Sparky*. Together with my son, Sam, we had a lot of fun.

My son Sam aboard Sparky at the Maritime Festival in Yarmouth IOW. About 2001

Often we were joined by Dave Harrison who lived close to Newtown Creek. At that time Dave was involved in photography. On a visit to the Isle of Wight in 2014 I learned that Dave had now developed a business shearing alpacas. In his younger days Dave had spent considerable time in the Falklands, where he became an expert sheep shearer. Another OGA sailor, Dave Randall, also sailed with me many times.

The annual Maritime Festival at Yarmouth on the Isle of Wight was a great favourite. In the last five years as a member of the OGA the Secretary was Jessica Warren and the President was the very well-known outstanding sailor and author, Tom Cunliffe. (Once, when racing with the OGA in his super Gaff Yacht Westerman, Tom got stuck on Black Rock off Yarmouth and had to wait until the tide lifted her off. Westerman was much faster than the rest of the smaller boats in the race and quickly passed most of them!)

Jessica Warren, the brilliant OGA Secretary, with her husband Mike on their yacht Roma. Right hand photo: the busy River Hamble near the Elephant Boatyard.

Mark Pooke (left) and Eduardo Brent, both good crewmen.

Rene Brent, with his family. From left: Geoffrey, Carmen, Rene's mother Janse, stepfather Roy, Rene, Silvia-Marie, Charles, and Eduardo. Circa 2010

The two presidents and secretaries I have mentioned were star performers, and the success and pleasure which the Solent Branch of the OGA gave to its members was in no small part due to them.

Most of my crossings from Poole to the Solent were uneventful. I do remember one of my early ones. On this occasion I had two RAF pilots from RAF Lyneham as crew. We set off fairly early in thick fog, having anchored for the night just off Brownsea Island. I hadn't got used to the set of the tides at this point. We cleared the Harbour entrance and set sail for Yarmouth. After about two hours the fog lifted and to my amazement we had only covered about a mile out of the 19 to Yarmouth. From then on I made sure that I studied the tide tables and got things right.

When Sam was my crew he always insisted in carrying more sail than was needed, resulting in *Sparky* sailing at an uncomfortable angle. I believe I am correct in saying that a vessel moves just as fast when sailing as level as possible. This was often a bone of contention! The crossings would have been far more enjoyable without this problem.

My last race with the OGA was a special one from Cowes to Lymington. About 30 Gaffers took part and the Solent was rough with winds Force 8 gusting to Force 10. John Richardson was my crew and we had a lady passenger, Kay Harris. It was the roughest conditions I have raced in, but also the greatest fun. Out of the 30 boats which lined up at the start, only six finished. Two were dismasted, one smashed its bowsprit and all the others retired. Luckily there were no casualties. *Sparky* was first in her class to cross the line and I was presented with a prestigious prize, which was an annual award. Known as the 'Gaffer's Eye', it was a very ancient telescope probably dating from Nelson's time. A very acceptable and appreciated prize!

Other cruises on *Sparky*

Over the 15 years I owned *Sparky* I made numerous crossings of the Channel, mainly to the Channel Islands and Brittany, and each time, either part of the passage or all of it has been a delight. This is especially so when you sail overnight, sometimes when it is pitch black. As dawn breaks, possibly at 0400 hours on a bright sunny morning, everything seems so wonderful. Another highlight of any voyage or passage is when you sight land. It is surprising the effect it has on the crew – and me. Quite uplifting!

Brest Ahoy – nearly!

I have covered my first venture across the Channel on *Sparky* with the two policemen. My next voyage was with my two young sons Sam, age15, and Joseph, 10, plus Chris Snelson, who answered an ad I placed in a sailing magazine. Chris was 16 years old but had had a lot of experience sailing with his dad, who owned a Gaffer which they sailed on the east coast. The fifth member of my crew was my very good friend and dentist, Tony Russell. Tony was a first class dentist. He was able to deal with my dental problems without injections, except for an extraction. He sailed with me on many occasions, although he never mastered the art of helming the boat. He was, however, a good cook and very good company, both for me and the boys.

Our plan was to head for the bi-annual Maritime Festival at Brest, off Cape Finisterre on the north-west point of Brittany. We set out quite early from Poole and had a steady crossing to Alderney. Negotiating the shipping lanes needs great care. The number of big ships plying the Channel is staggering and there is a continuous stream of them, in line and about half a mile apart . They have the right of way, although on one crossing a massive Swedish car carrier (no doubt full of Volvo cars and trucks) actually altered course for me, something that should never be relied upon!

Our first port of call was Braye Harbour on the northern point of Alderney. This is quite a large and busy Harbour which, in strong north/north easterly winds can be very rough. In extreme conditions it would be better to go about a mile to the west, towards the Casquets, and anchor in a sheltered bay just round the corner. This time we went straight into the main Harbour, as the wind was from the west. Previously I have been there in a strong northerly wind and it is most uncomfortable. The harbour wall needs extending! If you can get permission to go into the inner Harbour I would do so.

I had been to Braye numerous times and had got to know the owner of the Mainbrace Chandlery, Roland Neal RN, Engineering Officer Rtd.

Roland Neal RN Rtd - a truly great guy!

We were invited to have coffee at his home and later he installed some electrical equipment on *Sparky*. Alderney is a very friendly island and if I ever wanted to live in the Channel Isles I would choose it.

Leaving Braye next morning, our next stop was St Peter Port, Guernsey, where we spent one night and then headed straight for Brest, aiming to arrive in time for the festival. The distance to Brest from Guernsey would be approaching 100 miles. About halfway there we were battling against fairly strong westerly winds which cut our speed by half or more, 2-3 knots instead of 5-7. We were going to be too late for the festival, but Sam and Chris had made up their minds that they were going to get there come what may. We put into my favourite Harbour, Ploumanac'h, and Sam and Chris caught a train to Brest. Cheating really! I knew that Sam and Maggie Baylis would be there on *Brilleau*. Sam found them and they very kindly gave them a berth. Tony, Joseph and I had a very pleasant stay in Ploumanac'h, spending quite a lot of time in the Irish pub, where Tony and I enjoyed several pints of Guinness. For some reason the Guinness was as good there as you would get it in Dublin! Eventually our crew found their way back to Ploumanac'h and we set sail for home.

When we paid another visit to Guernsey, I attempted to find the anchorage at the south of the island which I had used previously with the two policemen. In total darkness this was impossible and I was forced to continue to St Peter Port, which we reached about 0200 hours.

Next evening I treated us to a special seafood supper in a local hostelry. Unfortunately this didn't agree with Tony's digestive system and he was proper poorly! As we left the next day the massive Condor Ferry from Poole was entering the small Harbour entrance as we were departing. We didn't argue with this twin hulled monster! We had another brief encounter with the same ferry a few days later.

The sail from Guernsey to Alderney was quite eventful and interesting. There was a super breeze blowing from the nor-nor east, about force 6, and we were making at least 7 knots. On that course we were heading straight for the southern tip of Alderney. To maintain the course on the eastern side of the island as I had intended a lot of tacking would have been required and progress would be much slower. I decided to make good use of the wind and head for the west of Alderney and then bear east for Braye at the northern end. There are several dangerous rocks on the westbound route, as there are all around the Channel Islands. Anyone contemplating sailing around the Channel Islands should make doubly sure they know where these rocks are. The west side of Jersey is the most treacherous. I made a careful and quick study of the chart and set a safe course, but in the rush I failed to take account of what the state of the tide would be once we reached the north of the island, where there is a row of rocks and small islands which forms a channel known as the Swinge, between them and Alderney. The first ones are the Casquets and the nearest one to Braye is Berhou, which has a large colony of puffins. We altered course for Braye and immediately the strong westerly tide took charge. Even with the assistance of the engine running flat out we were standing still, and without it we would have been going backwards. The tide had turned. Had we kept to the east of the island as the original plan, this would have been just right. We could now have been in serious trouble, sort of up the creek without a paddle!

I mentioned that I had a very good friend on the island, Roland Neal RN Rtd. On *Sparky*, I had two radios, one fixed above the navigation table and a hand-held one. Roland monitored his ship-to-shore radio continually during the day as he operated the Harbour water taxis. This was very fortunate. I called Roland, who immediately set a rescue plan in motion, not that we needed rescuing! Roland was a Rib enthusiast and often would drive his Rib to Southampton, about 80 miles, as a quite normal way of getting there. It had two 40 horsepower outboard engines. Roland was on the ball. His message was 'Stay where you are. I will drive my white van up on to the cliff above you and direct you into a safe anchorage'. Roland was very quick, and within 10 minutes he was just above us. Using his radio, he directed us into Crabby Bay. We dropped anchor and spent several pleasant days there, using our dinghy to get ashore. This anchorage was far more sheltered than Braye Harbour. On the eastern side there is a very large fort, probably built during the Napoleonic Wars.

In the morning of the second day of our stay, the Alderney lifeboat came into the bay on a training mission and anchored close by. Their timing was a couple of hours too early. Sam, who had spotted a few lobster pots, launched the dinghy and went over investigate. He returned with a lovely plump lobster. My reaction was that although I was tempted to eat it, it belonged to the person who owned the lobster pot. Reluctantly he set it free.

Shortly afterwards Chris began to complain of very severe pains which were worsening steadily, to the point where they were nearly unbearable. I called Alderney Coastguard and it was decided that Chris should be taken to hospital. The lifeboat was soon back again. A doctor jumped on board, nearly falling in the briny, and after examining Chris transferred him to the lifeboat. Later that day he was flown to Jersey Hospital and next day to his home in Bedford. This left us with my main crew missing.

Our stay in Alderney had one more highlight. My crew were now my two young sons, Sam and Joseph, and Tony Russell. To do some shopping from the anchorage it was necessary first to row ashore and then to walk a couple of miles overland to Braye. Tony and Sam went on this occasion. Sam, who was learning the ropes, tied the Tinker dinghy to a rock and off they went to re-victual *Sparky*. Meanwhile Joseph and I tidied Ship and took it easy listening to the Radio. After an hour or so, Joseph popped his head out of the hatch. With excitement in his voice he shouted down to me, 'The dinghy is being swept out to sea with the tide!' Within a few minutes it was indeed lost from view and heading towards New York!

Without a dinghy we would be in real trouble. Who could help us out? It is essential to have good friends all over the world, or at least make them as you go along. Knowing that Sam and Tony would be calling at the Chandlery, I gave Roland a call and outlined our predicament. 'Don't worry, I'll sort things out,' he said. He found Sam and Tony and in about half an hour or so, a cloud of spray rounded the headland. Under it were Roland and my crew.

By this time the dinghy had come back into view. The tide had turned, as it always does of course, and Roland brought it back in one piece minus an oar. That's what friends are for. It is not a good idea to tie a dinghy to a rock! Actually, I think Roland enjoyed our visit to Alderney and I have always made a point of seeing him each time I go there.

Roland was aware that at this stage of my sailing 'career' I was still an amateur. In all walks of life the more practice you get the more proficient you become, or should become! Roland, with the mass of experience he had had in the Navy, wanted to make sure that the weather for our return passage to Poole would be set fair. He monitored the forecasts with great care and after about three days he gave us the all-clear to set sail. For some reason he advised us to take the westward route through the Swinge, passing the Casquets. Normally, when returning to Poole, I would head due north from Braye. I did as Roland suggested and set off around 0700 hours. On Roland's route the distance would be at least 10 miles or so further than sailing direct north from Braye. All Channel crossings are affected by the tide, six hours going west and six hours to the east. One cancels out the other, and as long as you keep your heading pointing to your destination everything should fall into place.

As I have described, I had lost Chris and now had to be on watch continually myself or get Tony Russell to take a turn. Tony, as I have said, was a good cook, but he hadn't mastered how to steer a course using the compass. Whereas a passage from Alderney to Poole would normally take about 12 hours, by about 1600 hours we still had some 40 miles to cover. I let Tony take the helm several times during the first 10 hours and each time we were miles off course when I took over. By about 2000 hours, when I was due to have a break, I had just spotted the beam of the Portland lighthouse. I handed over the helm to Tony with the instruction to forget the compass and be sure to steer a course well to the right of this beam and when the beam from the Anvil lighthouse at Peveril Point near Swanage appeared, to keep well to the east of that as well.

Tony managed this very well and we made much better progress. The crossing probably broke all records. We took 17 hours instead of 12 and Sam and Joseph had a good sleep!

During the night the Condor ferry passed us at 40 knots. All we could see was a mass of spray. I called her up on the radio and enquired what the weather was like at Poole. They replied that it was fine and wished us a pleasant crossing. At 0500 hours we entered Poole Harbour and dropped the Anchor near Brownsea Island. By then I was knackered and needed some sleep. Tony, on the other hand, insisted on getting back to Calne, where he had dental appointments booked for that day. I persuaded him to cancel them. We all thoroughly enjoyed this holiday cruise and I, for one, learnt quite a lot.

A holiday cruise to Holland

Towards the end of 2004 I met Martin Pound, who had recently retired from the Royal Navy and now, when possible, spent most of the summer months aboard his yacht *Lucy*. Martin asked one day if I would like to accompany him on *Sparky*, with Sam and Joseph, on a cruise to Holland. I didn't need asking a second time! Over the winter months we planned the voyage, which would be in the school holidays. We agreed to be away for three weeks, the longest holiday I had ever had.

I arranged that Tony Russell would come on the first leg, Poole to Flushing, and Mike Shaw for the next seven days. This worked out very well and gave both Sam and Joseph an opportunity to get used to helping to sail *Sparky*. Holland is quite different to any other country. To live there you would require a boat and a bicycle – you could easily manage without a car. There is far more waterborne traffic than on the roads. Even the largest city, Amsterdam, is crisscrossed by canals.

Sparky at this time was moored in the River Frome at Ridge, near Wareham. I used the Ridge Marina as my base for parking my car and refueling etc. Later I moved *Sparky* to the Marina, where I always had good and friendly service. Martin, who was based in Gosport, agreed that we should meet up with him on *Lucy* at Flushing, where we would enter the Dutch canals.

We had a couple of setbacks at the start of our outward passage. Someone, it could have been me, dropped a mooring line over the stern which got round the prop, and it was impossible to remove it. Luckily we were alongside at Ridge Wharf, as the only solution was to lift *Sparky* out of the water to free the prop. This was dealt with very quickly by the Marina owner, Tony Clarke, and we were soon under way with a favourable tide. At low tide the River Frome is impassable.

We had a very fast sail to the Solent and beyond to Langstone Harbour, where we anchored close to Thorney Island for the night. Next morning we were ready to sail for our next port of call, Brighton, quite early. Sam started to lift the anchor and I was all set to go when one of my crew, I think it was Tony this time, dropped the main sheet over the stern, which got wound around the prop. Luckily it was not such a problem as the earlier one at Ridge. Sam dived over the side and was able to cut it free. We had anchored near Thornham Marina, so we paid it a visit and bought a replacement. Although our departure from Langstone was delayed, from then on, everything went with a swing.

We put in to Brighton Marina in the afternoon, with time to have a look round and get something to eat. Next morning we set sail for Boulogne. The crossing was largely in poor visibility and is quite tricky near the French and Belgian coasts. With care we arrived there at about 0200 hours. There were some Frenchmen partying on a large French Gullet and they agreed that we could tie up alongside them. Boulogne, which was previously a busy ferry Port, was looking a bit tired. The Harbour had silted up, leaving a very narrow channel. We were on schedule at this point and we next put in to Nieuport in Belgium. This proved to be much more inviting than Boulogne. It lies up a longish estuary and is well worth a visit.

We reached Flushing in daylight the next day and entered the Dutch canal system, which must be the most extensive in the world. It was the onset of the Dutch Maritime Festival, in which English gaff-rigged boats

Martin Pound RN Rtd. Brilliant single-handed
sailor and a great friend

Martin Pound sailing his gaff-rigged yacht Lucy, on
the Dutch canals

regularly take part. Martin Pound had arranged our entries and this
ensured that free moorings were reserved for us at each venue. These
festivals are mainly an opportunity for boat owners to socialize and make
new friends. It was a great start to a super sailing holiday.

Holland is quite an amazing country. A very large area has been
recovered from the sea by the construction of thousands of miles of
massive dykes which have been built up over several centuries. It is a
marvel of ingenuity, skill and hard graft. Until recently they wouldn't
have had the use of JCBs and the like, only hard graft. There's a saying,
'God made the world, but the Dutch made Holland'.

Initially the dykes were mounds or embankments which they made
by hand to protect their fields of growing crops. In more recent years
the main dykes have become massive and they not only keep out the sea
and control the flow of two great rivers, the Rhine and the Meuse, but
are built to carry motorways, including the Trans-European Highway.

The Dutch dykes carrying the Trans-European Highway

Martin had cruised the Dutch Canals at least once before and was familiar with the most suitable and interesting routes to follow and towns to visit. Our route took us via Vlissingen, Hellevoetsluis, Middelburg, Amsterdam, Dordrecht and Gouda by the cheese factory. We then entered the Marker Meer, where we anchored at Enkhuizen for one night and visited the very interesting museum. Next we passed into the Ijsselmeer (the northern part of what used to be called the Zuider Sea), which we left at Lemmer, heading for Harlingen. Here we spent a couple of days, during which we took the ferry to the Friesland Island of Vlieland. Martin, Sam and Joseph hired bikes and cycled right round the Island.

At this time I was suffering from my 'leaky valve' and I was very pleased with the help I had from Sam and Joseph. Joseph helmed the boat out into the North Sea, which was quite tricky. The North Sea is quite different from the English Channel. Visibility was poor, but with his good eyesight he was able to make sure that we kept within the marked channel. Being shallower, unless it is very rough, the waves are small, but there are many of them. We continued along the Dutch coast and entered the canal at Ijmuiden, leading to Amsterdam.

Sam and Joseph cycling around one of the Friesian Islands (Vlieland)

We spent a couple of days exploring this interesting city. While tied up in the marina opposite to the city we had a barbecue one evening in *Sparky's* cockpit and left the barbecue secured to the railings. Next morning it had gone! But don't let this put you off; generally the Dutch people are very friendly and helpful.

Sparky Leaving Harlingen. Skipper JW taking the salute. Note his three-week-old beard which took a week to remove! (It was like wire)

We now headed back into the North Sea and were on our way home. We put in to the fishing port of Scheveningen before passing the entrance to the Europort of Rotterdam. This is one of the busiest ports in the World; with huge vessels going in and out one after the other, so great care is needed. In several of the Dutch canals you have to be very careful to avoid the massive commercial barges which travel at great speed. They don't give way to pleasure craft!

A Dutch way of overcoming the housing problem!

All in all, a holiday on the Dutch canals is a great experience and definitely worthwhile, especially with one's family. You must have up-to-date charts and also a 'Pilot' book. I recommend the Imray Cruising Guide to the Netherlands. If you can go with someone who has been before, this is a great advantage.

Our next port of call, Martin Pound tells me, was Ostend. I have no memory of it but do know we spent a pleasant time in Calais. The 'boys', Martin, Sam and Joseph, had great fun on the bumper cars! After a day or two we headed out across the English Channel with a steady breeze and some sunshine. We had good views of the White Cliffs of Dover, Dungeness and Beachy Head, by which time it was getting dark. The adverse tide had slowed us down and when we were off Brighton it was pitch black. The lights of Brighton stretch for several miles and, at that time it was impossible, from about two miles off, to pick up the lights at the entrance to the marina. I called up the marina, but they weren't particularly helpful. Luckily I had one of Tom Cunliffe's pilot books, which stated that the entrance to the marina was 6 degrees west of Greenwich. We found that bearing and went straight in. It was about 2 am. We had a super sail back to the Solent, where we left Martin and Lucy, and by the evening we were safely back in Poole Harbour, having had a wonderful holiday.

Two final passages on *Sparky*

In late summer 2009 my crew was Dave Randall. Dave was, or had been, a member of the OGA. He was an experienced sailor, mainly along the south coast, especially the Solent, as he lived at Newtown Creek on the Isle of Wight. He sailed with me on numerous occasions. On this occasion we headed for Chichester Harbour, where at that time Nick Skeates had his Wylo propped up on the beach at Payne's boatyard at the top of Prinstead Bay.

The first Wylo sailed, and lived on, for 30 years by the designer and builder, Nick Skeates. Photo taken by JW at Payne's Boatyard in Chichester Harbour about 2009.

Dave Randall on the left with Nick Skeates. In the forecabin of his Wylo Nick stored his motorbike. This photo was taken at the launching ceremony of another Wylo 2, Apple.

Martin and Roma Morris's Wylo 2 "Apple", which they sailed across the "Pond", looking very smart in Yarmouth Harbour after a major overhaul 10 years after being self-built. Steel boats, whilst being extremely tough, need regular attention to avoid rust and corrosion. With regular care they will last for very many years. The general consensus is that the 32' version is the best.

It was a tricky passage to get to the boatyard. Apparently *Sparky* was the only Wylo II to have sailed there. While we were tied up alongside a pontoon the tide went out, leaving *Sparky* in thick mud. When we set sail with the tide we were unable to lower the lifting keel.

The wind was force 6 all the way back to the Elephant Boatyard on Southampton Water. *Sparky*, with a two-tonne keel beneath her, sailed beautifully, but getting the lifting keel to work again was a major problem. After a considerable effort with various tools at the top of the *Keel Housing* in the cabin, the only solution was to employ the 'elephant', the lifting equipment at the Elephant Boat Yard, which lifted *Sparky* out of the water with its 'trunk' and then blew gallons of water, again with her trunk, from underneath! The moral from this episode is that, when you are in a drying out Berth, leave the keel down by about 4 inches.

For the trip to Alderney we sailed from the Hamble River, calling at Yarmouth, where we tied up alongside by the Harbormasters' office and took on fuel and water. Early next morning we headed straight for Alderney and made about the fastest passage I remember. We took 11 hours to reach Braye Harbour. The original plan was to go on to a maritime festival at Paimpol. At this point we were on schedule and next morning we left with the tide and a fair wind. We were making 7 knots or more and very suddenly, bang, bang - we had hit a submerged rock, which was probably half a mile from the land near the Alderney Lighthouse. I should have taken more care when I studied my chart.

Fortunately, the boat wasn't holed like the liner *Costa Concordia*, but the rock had knocked the rudder off of the lower Pintle. With difficulty I was still able to steer, and we could have reached our next port of call, St Peter Port in Guernsey. However Dave panicked and worked himself into an almost uncontrollable state. To pacify him I called Alderney coastguard and they agreed to come to our assistance, which, in hindsight, was the most sensible thing to do. By the time they reached us I had sailed most of the way back to Braye. I let them tow us into the Harbour.

The following morning, the harbourmaster advised us to go into the inner Harbour so that when the tide was out we could inspect the damage and hopefully re-mount the rudder. The fishing boats use the inner Harbour, and one of the fishermen gave us some help to do the repair. He also gave me some sound advice which I will pass on - that is, when you sail from Braye going east, do not turn right until you have a clear view of the Swinge, the channel to the west of Alderney towards the Casquets.

By now we were too late for the festival at Paimpol. Luckily it was Alderney Week, so we decided to stay and enjoy the fun, which I can thoroughly recommend. At the end of the week we set sail for home, intending to make the crossing direct to the Needles. The wind was such that the best I could do was to make for Studland, where we anchored for the night. Next morning we had a lovely sail back to the Hamble and the Elephant Boatyard.

In 2012 *Sparky* was sold to Francis Douglas. Francis is restoring her to her original pristine condition and I am confident that she will give him many years of great sailing.

CHAPTER 14

A DOWNTURN IN MY LIFE

Five unpleasant years, 2005 to 2009

I had had a heart murmur for about 25 years, and in 2005 it became much worse. It proved to be a badly-leaking mitral valve. This became apparent when I was sailing from Poole to the Solent with an inexperienced crew and I was forced to do a lot of the heavy work, such as pulling up the mainsail. I saw a cardiologist and then a surgeon at Bristol Royal Infirmary (BRI) and it was agreed that I should have an operation to repair the leaking valve. Before having the operation I went on a cruise to Holland with Sam and Joseph in *Sparky* and Martin Pound in *Lucy*. I was glad I had two fit and capable lads with me, and we had a super holiday. (See Chapter 13.)

The next three years were the most unpleasant of my otherwise successful and happy life. It took two more open heart operations to sort out the problem. The first operation at the BRI repaired the faulty valve but led to me contracting MRSA, which attacked and ruined the repair. The cleanliness at that time in the BRI left a lot to be desired. A year later I was given a titanium valve, which I had done privately in a much cleaner private clinic, the Glen in Bristol. Unfortunately there was still a slight leak alongside the valve after this op, which made me pass out without warning. It took a three-month spell in the Queen Alexandra Hospital in Portsmouth before the cardiologist established the cause of my problem. I was sent to Southampton General Hospital for the third op and after a period of recuperation I have enjoyed very good health ever since.

Apart from regaining my health, the best thing worthy of mention is that apart from one failure at the Royal United Hospital in Bath and the poor standard of cleanliness at the BRI, I was very well looked after by all the National Health Service staff. I owe my life to them. Thanks to all of you!

Unfortunately my welcome on my return to Knights Marsh Farm after the first operation was quite negative. The developments over the next three years were quite unpleasant, to say the least. The situation became untenable and one morning in March 2007 I packed a bag and left. What followed is another story, to be told at a later date.

CHAPTER 15

IN THE SADDLE - HORSES AND HUNTING, 1936-1984

I was introduced to horses at the age of four. My father Henry, who would have been 30 or so at the time, bought an ex-warhorse called Tickity from Trowbridge Barracks. I vividly remember being led around the garden on Tickity's back. He was about 17 hands but very quiet and had seen many years as an army officer's charger. Father initially used a stable belonging to Alfie Crease, who lived about half a mile away at the bottom of Victoria Road in Trowbridge. Later he adapted his garage as a stable, which was more convenient. This was between the Waldens butter factory and his garden - it wouldn't be allowed today thanks to health and safety!

Father hunted Tickity with the Avon Vale. It wasn't long before Tickity grew too old for hunting however, and sadly he dropped dead while my father was riding him to hounds.

When I was about seven, Father bought me a grey pony called Theodore from a Judy Franks. I think it must have been in a circus. Frequently it would decide to have a roll with me on his back, usually

Henry Walden holding Tickity with Michael on board in front and John behind, 1938, at Downside, The Down, Trowbridge.

ending up in a puddle! This pony was kept at Hoopers Pool Farm., Southwick, near Trowbridge, the home of Wilfred Giddings and family before they moved to Melksham.

We didn't keep this pony very long, but it wasn't until I was in my teens that Henry bought the next one. This was a 15.2 hh Irish mare called Wendy. In the intervening years I regularly rode my cousin's New Forest pony, Topsy. My cousins were Gordon, Neville and Mary, the children of Wilfred and Hilda Giddings. Hilda was one of mother's sisters. I often stayed with them in the school holidays at Manor Farm, Sandridge, near Melksham.

While I was staying at Manor Farm at about the age of ten, Gipsies were frequently a problem. They would turn out their ponies at night into Wilf Giddings' fields to eat his grass. This was common thieving, and we set out to put a stop to it. One night Gordon, Neville and I hid in a ditch and waited until the Gipsies had departed. We then caught one of the ponies. The Gipsies moved on and didn't claim the pony, so she had a good home at Manor Farm. Topsy, as we called her, proved to be a fantastic pony and apart from some lessons I had while at Dauntsey's school, she taught me to ride. I remember the three of us on her back together galloping over a 40-acre field. When we came to a low hedge and ditch, the three of us landed in the ditch. Great fun! Fortunately it was a soft and dry landing.

The Irish mare, Wendy, was a useful animal, although a bit quirky. She could jump well when she decided to. One day, while practicing over some show jumps, instead of clearing a set of rails, she went underneath! I often rode her out into the countryside near Trowbridge and she loved jumping hedges and ditches. Taking part in Bromham Horse Show, the only way I could persuade her to go into the ring was backwards. Once in the ring she only knocked down one fence and came second!

The Irish mare, Wendy, at Bromham Show, JW on board, age 16, 1948

One of our family acquaintances at this time was Roger Hammond, who, with his father, owned one of the last cloth mills in Trowbridge to close. Roger was quite wealthy and took up hunting. In a short space of time he became the Master of the Wylie Valley Hunt and my brothers Michael, Ben and I were invited to have a day's hunting with them. Roger provided horses or ponies for both Ben and Michael and I rode Wendy. Ben and Michael had had minimal riding experience and when we set off at gallop over Salisbury Plain, Michael lost control. He hit a low branch of a big tree, came off his horse and was knocked unconscious. He survived, but this was the first and last time he got on a horse. He took up sailing instead.

Ben managed quite well and many years later, when he became quite wealthy, he became Master of the Avon Vale. I do know that he had quite number of bad falls!

In about 1947, Henry had purchased a very pleasant property on the edge of Trowbridge, Halfway Cottage, Hilperton Road, which had 10 acres of pasture and some outbuildings, including a couple of stables. When I was resting my horses, Henry would often look after them for me, which was always a great help. He loved my horses as much as I did. Riding out with my dad and sharing our interest in horses and racing was, I am sure, the best part of my long and eventful, Life.

Apart from working on the Canadian prairies (See Chapter 7) with a super pair of Percherons, there was, from about the age of 18, a gap in my riding 'career' which lasted until I was about 30 years old. In the meantime I took to the water. Henry didn't keep a horse during this period.

Roughly in 1960, Henry bought a good Irish cob, Chaser, and took up hunting once again. Shortly after, he offered me a day's hunting on Chaser. I had a fantastic day and was thoroughly hooked. Soon after that, Henry decided that if he had two horses we could ride out together. Debbie Hues, from Poulshot near Devizes, was advertising an Anglo-Arab gelding called Copper. We bought Copper between us. He was a useful horse, but not a nice one. I hunted him a couple of times, but he had a nasty habit of dropping his head when you landed over a jump, and once he unseated me, but he filled a gap.

Copper objected to being boxed. Once I managed to box him to the Boxing Day Avon Vale Hunt meet at Lacock, but he refused to be boxed for the homeward journey back to his stable at Trowbridge. I had to ride him the ten miles, which, after a hard day's hunting, didn't go down at all well! Debbie had some much better horses, including Pine Lodge, which won many point-to-points.

Among the well-known horsey families in the Avon Vale Country were the Maundrells at Calne. George Maundrell owned the Blackland

Stud at Blackland on the outskirts of the town. In my teens I remember that he had what was known as a 'travelling' stallion. This stallion would be taken to owners of mares which needed to be covered, a service which was widely used. If the mare to be covered was nearby the stallion would be walked there. Over longer distances they were either transported by lorry or, more often, by train.

George had a son, David, who was a successful rider in point to points. Sadly, at quite a young age David, who I knew quite well, had serious problems in his private life (probably partly his love life) which got the better of him. In addition his farming business was very seriously hit by an exceptionally violent hailstorm which destroyed the greater part of his crops, practically causing financial ruin. His father was a very hard taskmaster. Unfortunately David took his own life, which caused great sadness to his many friends including me. Anyone who has this type of problem should make sure, very quickly, that they get help.

Dick Strange was George Maundrell's stallion man and when Blackland Stud was sold he joined cousin Gordon Giddings. Dick was a great help in making Gordon's stud into a very successful enterprise.

Early on I formed the opinion that for 'private' use, mares are to be preferred to geldings. I have found that by and large they are kinder and they look after themselves and the rider. It is probably the mothering instinct. Where possible I have always kept mares. If you can't ride them for some reason, injury for example, you can always put them in foal, and this I have done on a number of occasions. A nice lady who hunted regularly with the Avon Vale once said to me 'The backside of a horse is good for the inside of your stomach', or words to that effect. I am sure she was right. Riding horses is one of the best things in the world for getting fresh air, keeping fit, meeting people and having fun.

When breaking in a horse, kindness and firmness must be the order of the day and this will pay dividends.

Around this time I had moved to Barn Cottage, Great Hinton, near Trowbridge, which had six acres of land. This enabled me to keep a horse, and I bought a very special unbroken three-year-old mare called Raspella, from Gordon Giddings, who now had a stud at Manor Farm, Sandridge. I had read several books about breaking in horses and set to work on Raspella, a thoroughbred cross Holstein. Her sire was Rasputin and her grandsire was Lester Piggott's second Derby Winner, Crepello. Raspella was quite a handful, but in about three months she came to hand and I was riding her to hounds. She was like riding two horses. If you showed her a jump, say 30 yards away, she would leap in the air and I knew we were going to clear the jump! Her main fault at this stage was that she would rear and several times she threw me out the back, even out hunting, which was embarrassing. Eventually she reared and knocked her head badly. She never reared again. Being too keen, I overworked Raspella while she was too young and she went badly lame.

It was noticeable that in the Trowbridge area there was a lack of good saddlers. During my travelling on business I often passed through Faringdon, where there happened to be one of the best saddlers for miles around, Stan Cooper. Stan was a Master Sadler par excellence. I became good friends with him and his family. Stan made two general purpose saddles for me and later a race saddle for point to pointing, and they were super.

JW on Raspella (at three years old), father Henry on Copper. In Michael's garden at Keevil, Circa 1968

The same garden 40 years later, minus the horses!

On one of my many travels over the UK I arranged to meet Tom Mayes, who owned Northampton Frozen Food Wholesalers, customers for Waldens' frozen pies. Tom, a rotund gentleman who was a farmer, also owned the restaurant in Buckingham where we met for coffee. Northamptonshire is noted for making good shoes and boots. At the time I was looking for a new pair of riding boots and Tom put me in touch with Edward Green. I was able to buy a special pair, made to measure, and, together with Stan's saddles and Edward's boots, I was very well equipped. Prior to that I was using Henry's old saddle and boots, and had worn them out!

I got on very well with Tom but there was a rather sad side to his life at that time. He and his wife had just parted and he had a huge problem in dividing up his very valuable properties. I think he bought the restaurant so that he could be well fed!

I was lucky to have very good blacksmiths, including Ivor Smith (husband of Betty, my first secretary at Waldens) from Steeple Ashton and Ken May from Calne. Wendy Barnes, Lynn Rooke, Sue Telfer and Rebecca Godwin helped me with my horses and the other animals I kept, mainly sheep, but also calves which we raised and sold as stores.

On one day's Hunting, Raspella (when still a three year old), unknown to me, stepped on a sharp piece of porcelain china which penetrated her front left hand hoof. At that time it was difficult for the vet (Richard Geering) to diagnose the cause of the lameness. It only became apparent when a small hole appeared in the top of the hoof and pus began to run out. With the use of bran poultices in a special poultice boot the offending foreign body came out too. This was a great relief for me, and even more so for Raspella, who had suffered a lot of pain.

A hunting farmer, Arthur Corp from Edington, advised me not to hunt Raspella as a three-year-old and said I should let her mature until she was five. I took his sound advice and took her to Gordon's stallion, Dairialitan, to get her in foal. Unfortunately the foal was stillborn. At five years old I was hunting her again and she was fantastic. By this time I had moved to Knights Marsh Farm, where the riding country at that time was superb. The farm was just under the Marlborough Downs and it was ideal for getting a horse fit, especially climbing Heddington Hill, which was nearly a mile long. I got Raspella 100% fit and rode her in several point-to-points.

By now I was 40 years old, which is a bit late to start riding in point to points – most riders start when they are about 17 years old, even 16! However I had some great rides, the last one being in the Beaufort Hunt point to point over the course at Didmarton. Unfortunately on the second circuit, when well placed, Raspella broke down, lame again. This time it was very serious and I had to have her put down. This practically broke my heart and it took me some time to get over it.

Here are one or two useful tips about feeding and avoiding illness in horses and ponies. When feeding a very highly-strung horse, such as Raspella, who couldn't cope with oats in her feed, change to boiled barley and linseed plus sugar beet. This provides more than adequate energy and I thoroughly recommend it. It is essential that feeding is balanced with the amount of work that horses and ponies have to do. Many ponies are unable to cope with too much very rich grass, which will cause laminitis. Keeping fetlocks and hooves free of mud is essential to avoid mud fever. Another very painful illness which should be avoided at all costs is azoturia, which is caused by an imbalance between feed and work. The main symptom is that the animal's muscles seize up and it has great difficulty in moving. It will also be in severe pain. With minimal or no work, cut the feed down. Dancer was inflicted with this when I was riding her out. She was in excruciating pain and unable to move. I had to get someone to collect us with the Land Rover and horse box.

Meanwhile, I had bought several other horses, mainly from Gordon. One in particular was a thoroughbred mare called Dairidance, by

Dairialitan. This one I called Dancer and she was 15.3 hands high (Raspella was 16.3 HH). She was three years old, and rather than working her too early I broke her in and then put her in Foal. She had two foals. The first one, by New Member, had a slight heart murmur. I broke her in, but often when I was riding her she would collapse, which was disconcerting to say the least! I sold her to someone who was aware of the trouble but wanted to breed from her.

Dancer's second foal was quite special. She was by another of Gordon's thoroughbred stallions, Royal Smoke, and we called her Stockley Tornado. I put her in training as a two-year-old (sharing the cost with John Tarrant, who was at school with me, both at Dauntsey's

JW competing at Larkhill Hunter Trials on Dairidance (Dancer), 1978

THE PROVEN STALLION

DAIRIALATAN

BAY 1955

Winner of 20 races under J.C. & N.H. Rules

Standing at:—
G. W. GIDDINGS,
Manor Farm Stud,
Sandridge,
MELKSHAM, Wiltshire.
Telephone : Melksham 702277

Dairialatan, sire of Dairidance (Dancer)

and Westholm in Andover) to race on the flat. With a better trainer she would have been brilliant. She did come second at Windsor. When I took her home I schooled her over fences and hunted her. She was super like her Dam, Dancer, who was outstanding. In hindsight, I wish I had raced Stockley Tornado over fences. Dancer (Dairidance) was a half-sister to the Queen Mother's racehorse, Special Cargo, which had won many steeplechases, notably the Whitbread Gold Cup at Sandown in 1984. Special Cargo was such a star performer and such a great favourite with racegoers that there is now a statue of him at Sandown.

When possible I hunted once or more per week, both with the Avon Vale and the Beaufort, whose boundary was close by on the other side

Another of Gordon's stallions, New Member, sire of many National Hunt winners.

HRH The Princess Royal presenting Gordon Giddings with 'Lifetime in Racing' award, 2011. Well deserved!

Gordon with some of his young stock

232

JW competing on Stockley Tornado at Larkhill. She still thought she was racing and was 'carting' me around the course. She hit the next jump, a solid bank built of sleepers, and we retired.

A Sprinter who stayed a mile.

ROYAL SMOKE

BAY 1966

by ROYAL SERENADE—
HICKORY SMOKE by
AMBIORIX

This handsome American bred
impressive performer has retired
sound to stand at

G. W. GIDDINGS,
MANOR FARM STUD,
SANDRIDGE,
MELKSHAM,
WILTSHIRE.
Telephone: Melksham 702277

Royal Smoke, the sire of Stockley Tornado

Two fantastic horses: Stockley Tornado and Dairidance (Dancer)

of the A4 from Knights Marsh Farm. This used up most of my holiday entitlement – I preferred hunting to holidays and I believed in delegating my work whenever possible! Usually the hunting season lasted from the 1st of November until mid-February, depending on the weather. It paid to hunt as much as possible before Christmas.

At this time my children, Hugh, 14 and Sarah, 10, took up riding and I was able to buy them each a pony. Hugh's was called Rolly and this one proved to be ideal for him. He had been hunted with the Avon Vale and was a great Jumper. Hugh was lucky to be taken to several Beaufort Hunt meets by Terry Huband with his daughter Jane and Kathleen Welch. Kathleen's Dad, Michael Welch, sold me my first tractor and other farm machinery when I first arrived at Knights Marsh Farm.

The other pony I bought was from Terry's father, Walter Huband, for Sarah. This one was called Nicky. It was a Palomino and had been a great Show jumper. Nicky was a super pony but proved to be too much for Sarah, who wasn't ready for him. In a thunderstorm on the Downs he ran away with Sarah and this put her off riding. My fault, I guess! Luckily Sarah wasn't hurt. It is no good to be over horsed!

Terry Huband's brother Keith had a big grey ex-showjumper called Fag Ash and I often rode out with them. Later I had a 15.1 HH called Roman (by Roman Candle, another of Gordon Giddings' stallions). Hugh hunted Roman, who was, like Copper, awkward! Riding to an Avon Vale Meet at Bulkington he dropped Hugh into a water-filled ditch. In spite of this, Hugh still had a good day's hunting! We shared Roman with my father, who did his best to school him to pull a trap. I think Henry rushed things, as he ran away with him and tipped him out. Henry was not wearing a helmet and was hurt quite badly. I was one of the first riders in the Avon Vale to wear a chinstrap to prevent my hat from coming off if I had a fall. Luckily I had very few falls, but when I did my hat always stayed on and I never had a serious head injury. I expect you will have noticed that most of the horses which gave me problems were geldings!

Hugh had stolen a march on me and hunted with the Beaufort before me. Fortunately I had an introduction to the Joint Master of the Beaufort Hunt, Major Gerald Gundry, who, in his younger days had lived in the same Dorset village as my Aunt Marion, another of Mother's sisters.

I was made very welcome on Thursdays when they hunted in the Calne area. Many of those hunting on a Thursday were farmers and I had a lot of fun. If the fox was fit he would beat the hounds. Foxes are cunning devils and will kill poultry for fun if given the chance. When they move into urban areas they are a menace and a health hazard. They have been known to attack babies.

Marion Brunt with her terrier, Snuffer. At the time when Marion knew Gerald Gundry she was Mrs Honeyben and lived at Chilfrome in Dorset.

Hounds needed a good sense of smell to keep on the trail. If the fox was getting old and not so fit, the hounds did their job practically instantaneously. In 20 years I never witnessed any cruelty. Hunting for farmers was part of their way of life, just as football is for a large section of society. Long may it continue!

The Secretary of the Beaufort was Major Ronny Dallas. A fine man; In WW2 he had been a POW in Japan and was lucky to be alive. He was still suffering. Among the farmers were Derek Rose, Robin Pocock, Alan Hutchings, John Mowlem, Eric Smith, Douglas White and his son John, who became a Field Master, and Dick Horton, also a Field Master. I was honoured to have their company and friendship. The super Huntsman throughout this time was Brian Gupwell.

Five good men and true, Hunting farmers: Alan Hutchings, Eric Smith, Robin Pocock, John Mowlem and Dereck Rose, all regulars with the Beaufort Hunt on Thursdays

Over nearly 20 years I hunted various horses, notably Raspella, Dancer and Stockley Tornado. All three were super, but Dancer was the best. I was very fortunate, as I had horses as good as any in both hunts. Dancer, with others, would often lead the field with the Beaufort. On one occasion the Master's horse refused to jump a fairly wide brook and Dancer gave him and the field a lead. In seven seasons I did not have a fall and jumped everything in sight. On one occasion, Tornado jumped a very high metal five-bar gate which everyone else avoided. Dancer would jump great hedges and ditches, one after the other, even with wire either side.

One day, with the Beaufort, a fox was put up near Bremhill and the hunt followed, jumping hedge after hedge, about six in a row. The fox got away. Half an hour later another one was a put up from the same cover and ran in the same direction over the same line of hedges, and we followed. The farmer wasn't at all pleased and the hunt was banned from his land forthwith. The spoilsport!

The 'Thursday country' in the Beaufort I shall always remember as the 'happy country', especially as it was so well patronized by the very friendly local farmers. The most popular Meets were at Bushton, Bremhill, Hilmarton, East Tytherton, Compton Bassett, Seagry, Dauntsey and Cliffe Pypard.

On one occasion, when out with the Avon Vale riding Raspella, the Field Master, a rather pompous person, stopped and dismounted at a gate on a bridge over the Kennet and Avon Canal. I was close behind him and had no chance of stopping Raspella, and we jumped the Master's horse and the gate. My friend, Tom Breach, failed to apply the brakes and ended up in a heap on the canal bank! He was lucky he didn't have a dipping. One fellow attempted to jump Worton Brook where it was quite wide and promptly landed in the middle!

The Huntsman of the Avon Vale at that time was Neal Parker, and he provided some great sport. The Master of the Avon Vale was Major John Bartholomew, Chairman of Wadworth's Brewery in Devizes, famous for 6X beer. Another prominent Wiltshire hunting family were the Fullers at Neston, who were connected to the brewers Fuller, Smith and Fuller of Chiswick, famous for London Pride. There was some very good hunting country in the Avon Vale, especially around Worton, Bulkington, Marston, Poulshot, Steeple Ashton, Seend, Cumberwell near Bradford on Avon, Lacock and even Heddington, near where I lived at Knights Marsh Farm. Neal Parker signed a form which confirmed I was capable of riding in Point to Points. He also advised me to school Raspella over the practice fences at Larkhill Racecourse, which I did.

I did buy one non-thoroughbred horse, a roan cob called Sergeant, and he was a useful hunter, often hired for a day's hunting by Ken Hutchings from Calne, father of Alan mentioned above.

I competed in many hunter trials including the Tedworth, Wilton, South and West Wilts, several at Larkhill and Kingsclere and one at

Crudwell. The latter was at the home of Lord Oaksey, who opened his personal practice steeplechase fence for me to jump with Dancer. Another special one with Dancer was at the School of Infantry, Warminster, run over a jolly good course on Salisbury Plain. One of the jumps on this course was in and out of a narrow lane which had a stone wall each side. Dancer approached it too fast and Instead of jumping out she came to an abrupt halt against the outgoing wall. I rolled out over her neck and landed on the wall. Each jump on a hunter trial course has to have a steward and this particular jump was 'manned' by a very attractive lady, Christine Hart. She helped me remount and I finished the course in good time. I became good friends with Christine and her husband John, who was a Major in the Army, stationed at Warminster.

I also competed with Raspella and Tornado and was often fortunate to have the company of Lt. Col Bob Huskinson, who had retired from the Royal Artillery. He was a marvellous horseman and was still competing in hunter chases well into his eighties. I held a hunter trial at Knights Marsh Farm in 1973, and Bob took part. At the last fence, a fixed five-bar gate, Bob's horse didn't look where he was going. He hit the gate and went flying. Bob knocked out several teeth and damaged his shoulder. From that day he was unable to lift his right arm above his shoulder! In spite of this, we became great friends and remained so until he passed away at the ripe old age of 93.

Bob was born and grew up in India, where his father was serving in the British Army. Bob joined the Royal Artillery as a boy bugler at 14 years old. Early in WW2 Bob was in the British Expeditionary Force in France and was evacuated from Dunkirk. Later he served in Burma, fighting the Japanese. He was a marvellous horseman and a great friend.

Princess Anne came to the hunter trials, but she decided that the course was too wet to risk her very valuable eventer. Some time after, I often met the Princess out hunting on a Thursday with the Beaufort. She was always very pleasant, like most people I met when hunting with them. I had a number of days hunting with the Tedworth, which was

*Bob Huskinson
on holiday in
sunny Spain*

Bob in action at Larkhill on Sona

well supported by members of the Guinness family. The Master was
Peter Horton. It is amazing the fun which can be had with a good horse,
even hacking out, especially with good company.

Another pleasant activity was taking part in charity rides. One
particular one I entered with Raspella started at East Kennet and
covered at least 15 miles over the Pewsey Downs. I believe there were
about 80 fences to be jumped if you wanted to, and Raspella jumped
all of them!

I had constructed 18 fences on the 70 acres of Knights Marsh Farm
and those who took part in the hunter trials enjoyed themselves. The

commentator at the trials was Lord Oaksey, who as John Lawrence had won the Grand National on Cromwell. Many well-known National Hunt jockeys competed, such as Richard Pitman (famous for riding Pendil and Chrisp) and we raised a useful sum for the charity, the Injured Jockeys' Fund. Running a hunter trial required many volunteer helpers, mainly to act as stewards at fences. Afterwards one or two approached me asking to be paid. I had barely broken even, so this was not possible. It put me off running hunter trials. One was enough! Fortunately I did have plenty of volunteer helpers, who included my friend Fred Poynter and his wife Renee. My wife Ann was in charge of the catering and Bill Pitt from the Ivy provided the bar. Generally it was very successful.

The horse in the above photo I called Plane Sam. Marion changed the name to Okeechobee. On a visit to her farm in Kent, Marion and I rode out on the sands close by. I was on Okeechobee. He put his front feet in some quicksand and was sinking rapidly. Not a funny situation. I managed to dismount and avoid the quicksand and, one way or another, extricated Okeechobee. Watch out for quicksand!

A useful gelding I bred. Sold at Ascot sales to my cousin Marion Brunt

When in about 1984 I discovered that I had a heart murmur, I was told I shouldn't do anything likely to strain my heart. I took the advice, and this ended my days with horses. I now live on my memories, which are fantastic! In my younger days I had read a very good book, 'Memoirs of a Fox Hunting Man' by Siegfried Sassoon. This had fired my imagination. Sassoon had a lot of fun and so did I. I recommend his book. Sassoon is famous as a First World War soldier and for his poetry – he lived at Heytesbury near Warminster.

I frequently attended race meetings, mostly with my father and Bob Huskinson. These included the Cheltenham Gold Cup, when Arkle won, and again when Desert Orchid did likewise. Others included a day out at 'Glorious Goodwood' with Fred and Renee Poynter, the Epsom Derby and days at Newbury and Ascot. I was also lucky enough to go to Aintree for the Grand National. This time the great Red Rum was second. Afterwards I went to Southport, where Red Rum was trained and was taken into his stable with his owner and trainer, Ginger McCain. At that time Ginger only had Red Rum, and kept him in a stable right next to his house. Ginger got Red Rum fit on the Southport sands, whereas I got Raspella fit on Heddington Hill. Both did the trick!

Just a word of warning. As in all walks of life, there are good and bad in the horse fraternity. If you are buying a horse or pony for the first time, always have a second opinion before you part with your money and, if possible, have the animal on trial for at least a week. Engaging a vet is sensible. A horse or pony which walks out well is a good sign.

All Horses which are in work in the winter months are normally clipped out, either partially or full. On one occasion I had the doubtful help of young lass who helped me with my Horses. She offered to help with the clipping of Dancer. Very quickly, she dropped the electric clippers on the concrete floor. Dance promptly stepped on the cable and had a violent electric shock. That was the last time I was able to clip Dancer unless I had the vet, who immobilized her. I did this a couple of times. Not only was it very expensive but it was also most unpleasant for both me and Dancer. Risky too!

As a hobby, I can truthfully say that horses and ponies have given me as much pleasure, or more, than any other activity. In my life with horses I have preferred to ride them as much as possible rather than keeping them for racing. It is not easy to do both unless you have unlimited funds. For me riding them was much the best!

Since moving from Knights Marsh in 2007 I have lived closer to the sea and have concentrated on sailing. Once a countryman, always a countryman! I was fortunate to meet Lionel Veck and his family, who kept several horses and ponies which they used to compete in driving competitions (like the Duke of Edinburgh). I went with them sometimes, mostly in the New Forest. This was quite exciting. Both Lionel and his daughter Sally were experts.

The Hurley Hambledon Hunt was the local foxhound hunt, and one of my doctor friends, David Ibbotson in Bishops Waltham, was a keen follower.

Lionel Veck and his daughter Sally on a pub crawl with JW

David Ibbotson on his favourite hunter, Jimmy. Both photos 2009

A meet of the Avonvale Hunt at The Bell, Broughton Gifford, 1985. In the foreground is the Hunt Master, Ben Walden, with his daughter Emma. Phyllis Walden, mother of John, Michael and Ben, is on the right of the picture following on foot.

CHAPTER 16

ADVENTURES ON THE ROAD, 1949-2014

Cars, motorbikes, driving, speed limits and accidents

Over the years I have had numerous cars, some good, some bad and some indifferent. Generally, if they have performed reliably, I have kept them for three years before changing to a new one. Not many stood up to the work that I gave them.

My first car in 1949 was a super MG TD. As I decided to go to Canada this was sold after two years without a blemish. Whether this was luck or good driving I am not too sure. This would be unusual for new drivers in later years.

My first car, an MG TD, 1950 (part of the Walden factory behind)

One fairly early car I had was a Lotus Elan, which was not just dangerous but lethal. At that time they were made of glass fibre, which, as I was soon to discover, had no strength whatsoever. This one would easily reach 100 mph between Yarnbrook crossroads (now a roundabout) and West Ashton crossroads. I nearly ran out of road!

A Lotus Elan. Fortunately mine had a hard top, although not hard enough!

On a business trip to Eastleigh, near Southampton, in my first Elan, I stopped at some traffic lights. When they turned green I went slowly ahead and noticed that a Co-op artic was coming round the next bend too fast and beginning to jack knife. I was in its path and to avoid it I mounted the left hand pavement. The driver didn't stop and the rear wheels of the trailer passed straight over the Elan. I ducked! The Elan completely broke up. My left leg was bent backwards and I had a nasty cut on my forehead which needed stitching at Southampton General Hospital. I was lucky to be alive! Brother Michael collected me from Southampton and I was back to work next day.

The Elan was replaced by Rob Walker's Garage at Corseley, near Warminster. When it was due for its first service it was collected by one of RW's staff, who promptly skidded on some cow dung and crashed into a wall at Corseley, writing it off! I was using the Elans for business so that I could get around quite quickly and I also had a Singer Gazelle estate for sensible family use. Father insisted that I had a more robust vehicle and an Audi saloon was purchased. This was quite good, but the gear change was on the steering column and it very quickly fell apart.

The Audi was followed by an MGB, which was good. I had a couple of minor accidents in this. One was on Hanger Lane on the North

Circular Road in London. Traffic was very heavy and moving slowly, as was often the case in London at that time. The road was covered in leaves and, being wet, was very slippery. Suddenly some idiot drove out of the queue of traffic about 50 yards ahead, straight into a car coming from the opposite direction. I braked and skidded into the car in front. There was quite a lot of damage and the car was immobile. On another occasion on the Hammersmith Flyover the traffic stopped and I didn't! I went home by train both times. I was still quite new to driving in London and I am sure I have taken greater care since. Experience makes a difference.

Additionally, someone crashed into me who was driving far too fast on a sharp bend in a narrow lane close to my home at Great Hinton, near Trowbridge. Fortunately my young son was strapped in. I was OK but Hugh suffered a ricked neck. At that time safety belts weren't compulsory but, luckily, I had been using them for a couple of years at least.

The MG was followed by a Rover V8 and then a Triumph Stag. Both of these gave mechanical trouble (engines) and were unreliable. I then had my first Alfa Romeo, one of nine over the years. Apart from one which was a 'rust bucket' and jumped out of second gear, the others were fantastic and never let me down.

In my early days of driving there was far less traffic and with a good car it was possible to cover great distances at quite high speeds in safety. Quite often I would leave Trowbridge early in the morning, say 6 am, be in Liverpool or Manchester for a meeting at nine and then be home in time for tea! On one particular trip to Cumbria lasting three days, I had completed my business in Carlisle at 12 noon. By 3 pm precisely, I was in Chippenham. This was in an Alfa Romeo similar to the one pictured below. The traffic was minimal and I was driving according to the road conditions.

Alfa Romeo Giuliettas, 1960

In the late 70s I had cause to go to London to meet Leon Brittan QC, who was at one stage a Government Minister, but then practicing as a barrister. I was accompanied by my friend and solicitor, Tony King. We completed our business in London around teatime and headed for home. I was driving at a sensible speed within the limit when out of the blue a sports car passed me at great speed. I was interested to know what sort of car it was so I accelerated and got closer to it. It was an Austin Healey. As it approached the exit for Thatcham, without warning, it swung off the motorway (the M4) towards the exit to the A4 then turned right round and came across the motorway, straight into my path. We were in the middle lane and it was impossible to avoid a crash. This was a major accident.

Fortunately, neither Tony nor I were hurt (seat belts saved the day again) and we were able to extricate ourselves from the car, which was a write-off. One of us got to the side of the road and the other to the central reservation, where we tried to wave down the approaching traffic which rapidly piled up, and a number of people were hurt.

Very quickly the police were on the scene, plus three ambulances and two fire engines. Almost like a battlefield! The other driver was unhurt. The police interviewed him first and accepted his version, which was that I had caused the accident. This was quite untrue. The police gave me a notice of intended prosecution. My speed at the time of the accident was less than 70 mph.

In time I had a summons to attend court. However, just before the due date the local police came to see me with the news that the other driver had owned up. Apparently he had been to a party and had had a few drinks. When the crash happened he had momentarily dropped off to sleep and this was the cause of the accident. The guilty driver was not the owner of the car but a salesman for the company which owned it. He had been trying to save his job. I was completely exonerated.

Apart from the Alfas I have had one or two other cars, including a Mercedes A300 Diesel. This was too big and didn't suit me. Alfas have proved to be the best for me. Over the years I have collected a few points, most of which have been for minor infringements such as parking in a spot which had become a no-parking area overnight. The fellow who issued the parking ticket had recently left Waldens, where he had, for a short time, been a driver. Not a very good one! This parking spot was in Church Street, Trowbridge and was quite suitable for parking. The Council was out to make money at drivers' expense and inconvenience.

At one time my points totted up so that I was banned from driving for three months. Apart from that I have driven for two spells of twenty years without any points at all. Once, in about 2009, I was caught doing

Alfa Romeo GTV6 (not as good as the Brera or the Giuliettas!)

38 in a 30 mph limit and elected to accept a higher fine, £70 instead of £60, and take a driver awareness course. This proved to be quite sensible. All in all, my approach to driving is to drive according to the road conditions, which I have done, and still do. If everyone did that there would be far fewer accidents.

My latest Alfa Romeo Brera 2014. Reliable, comfortable, very roadworthy and one of the most attractive cars on the road. The Italians have a great flair for design.

In time I changed from petrol-driven vehicles to diesel. Over the years diesel fuel had been improved substantially, to the extent that the performance gap between petrol and diesel-powered vehicles has practically been wiped out. There are other very important advantages – no spark plugs are required or carburetors, which were often troublesome, particularly in in the early petrol cars or trucks. In addition, petrol is a fire hazard and quite a number of accidents have resulted in drivers and passengers being burnt to death. Diesel is safer because it needs far more heat to ignite, whereas petrol is instantaneous. For me, this was a good enough reason to change to diesel and I have not regretted it for one moment. When you make the change, make sure you put the correct fuel in, otherwise you won't be going anywhere! After making the change it is very easy to make that mistake, as I know to my cost and the hole in my pocket. CO_2 emissions from diesel engines have been greatly reduced in recent years, but possibly not enough!

During the 60s there was a very serious fuel shortage and motorway police were instructed to enforce a 50 mph speed limit. I was travelling as usual and when homeward bound on the M1 I caught up with a slow moving queue of traffic. Slowly, I overtook them until I drew level with the police car, which was doing precisely 50 mph. I thought I would overtake the police car at 51 mph. The policeman opened his window and with a loudhailer told me to keep to 50. I didn't have any choice!

Sometime around 2008/9 I was beginning to feel a bit fed up with having to drive at 30 mph in many areas where it would safe to drive at 40/45 mph, especially in a good car. I had the idea that the speed limits should be treated as advisory limits and that drivers should drive according to road conditions, something which I had been doing for years. I took the trouble to set out my thoughts in a document which I handed in to the Chief Constable of Wiltshire at their HQ in Devizes. Apparently it was circulated to all Chief Constables and to the Secretary of State for Transport, who duly wrote to me. They were quite helpful and, generally, with some reservations, I accepted their views. The text of the document is shown below. Possibly some of its content is somewhat extreme, but they were my thoughts at that time.

I am pleased to note that the standard of training and regular testing of vehicles has greatly improved. Before closing this chapter I hope that the police will concentrate on catching motorists who are obviously not driving according to road conditions and desist from catching those who may be slightly exceeding the speed limit but are driving according to the road conditions. In the past, many police – fortunately, not all – have been notorious for catching as many drivers as possible, possibly aiming at promotion or just 'for the hell of it'. By and large this has not contributed to road safety but has simply extracted money from very many careful drivers who would not be the cause of accidents. I sincerely hope that the powers that be take careful note of my proposals regarding advisory speed limits.

Frequently I have considered the question of fixed speed cameras and my view is that they do nothing to improve safety. I have noted that drivers who are driving at a sensible and safe speed often brake rapidly once they spot a speed camera to ensure they will pass it at the designated speed and then accelerate once they have passed it. This has been known to cause accidents. They should be got rid of altogether.

Recently 'community speed cameras' have been introduced. The local residents who use them are suitably attired with bright yellow jackets which can be seen at a distance, which gives the drivers a chance to keep to the limit. This is acceptable. If fixed speed cameras had a bright yellow warning sign on the approach this would have the same effect and would also be acceptable. As they are at present, July 2014, they are just a means of making money.

Solar-powered warning signs are very effective. When sited just inside the 30 mph limit they act as a polite reminder that you are going slightly too fast. It is possible that you were distracted as you passed the limit. These should replace fixed speed cameras.

Below is the document I delivered to the Chief Constable of Wiltshire. This has been considerably updated over recent years.

March 2009
Time to review outdated speed limits

Aim at responsible driving. Teach responsible driving. Only allow responsible drivers.

Enshrine the word responsible in the ethos of driving tuition, rules of the road, the Highway Code.

Many current speed limits are unnecessary. You expect a limit in built-up areas where children and older people are present and at certain times of the day. Responsible drivers would be aware of this. Frequently there are limits in non-built-up areas where it is quite safe to drive at up to 40 or 50 mph with modern cars driven by responsible drivers. It should not be allowed for stupid people, who probably can't or don't drive, to get up a petition and get a limit added where it is obviously not needed, or is, most likely, the incorrect limit.

Drivers should be able to drive at speeds according to the road conditions. If they don't then they should not be allowed to drive. All learners, once they have passed their test (or before) should be subject to a suitability test to establish if they are responsible and accept that they should drive according to the road conditions. It should take account of their age, attitude, the type of vehicle they will be driving etc., Can they read? This should cut out 'boy racers' and irresponsible immature persons who should not be allowed to drive in the first place. Irresponsible/bad drivers should be reported to the police and they should be retrained or banned.

There should be an overall policy to determine advisory speed limits where this is necessary.

Many roads are now shown at 50 mph and generally this is correct. It could be shown as an advisory limit, which responsible drivers would respect. This should be applied generally.

Drivers should be more considerate and give way to others more at junctions i.e. filter more.

In time, mandatory speed limits could and should be replaced by advisory limits. Calming features, generally, are very sensible. Not speed cameras. Solar-powered signs advising drivers to slow down are good and helpful. The majority of the current mandatory Speed Limits could be reclassified as Advisory Limits.

Area trials should be carried out.

In a reasonable time the amount of police time wasted on enforcing outdated speed limits would be reduced. Accidents would also be reduced. The relations between the motorist and the police would improve. Insurance claims and costs would be lower.

Food for thought, discussion and action!

The writer has driven for over 60 years (including HGV Class 1) and has, where possible, driven according to the road conditions, and has never been the cause of a serious accident. Generally, in many places, mandatory speed limits are rubbish. Advisory speed limits are the system to aim for. I drove for two periods of 20 years without any points and I didn't hang about!

There should be a minimum educational standard before anyone should even consider driving, even with L Plates.

If the basic standards are enforced this will reduce the number of cars on the road by possibly 10% and thereby reduce carbon emission.

The high level of insurance being applied to young drivers indiscriminately is quite stupid. Not all youngsters are irresponsible and the testing process should take far more account of this, possibly awarding the new driver points out of 10 which could be reflected in the level of insurance to be established. This could be divided into categories A, B and C. The higher the category the lower the premium. For example, I had two sons who were as different as Chalk from cheese. The younger one, Joseph, approached everything in calm and measured way, whereas his brother, Sam, was completely opposite. In Sam's case everything *had to be done at maximum revs. Sam couldn't get enough of speed and at the prime age of 29 he crashed his motorbike into another car in Belgium and was killed instantly. I would have categorized Joseph as A or even AA, whereas Sam would be C, or at least to have been given extra training. Both boys passed the driving test first time, as I did.*

This leads me to an anti-social problem with motorbikes. By and large, most motorbike riders are responsible, similar to car drivers. However, quite a large number are rather like my son Sam, and insist on driving at maximum revs wherever they are. As a case in point, I was driving along the A36 from Warminster to Salisbury recently and all of a sudden, without warning, there was a massive noise, like an explosion, and three powerful motorbikes at maximum acceleration flew by, probably at 70 mph, and frightened the life out of me. I class this as a form of anti-social behaviour which is much worse than being slightly intoxicated. The powers that be - Parliament, not Brussels - should give this matter some serious consideration. Hundreds of motorbike rider, who drive as I have described are killed on the roads each year. It is time that some action is taken to avoid this unnecessary loss of life, which costs large sums of taxpayer's money, police time, the NHS etc., in addition to the awful grief which the affected families have to endure.

The police should cultivate a friendlier approach to motorists. So should those who hand out parking tickets. In fact, a change of culture!

Since completing this chapter I have been caught by a fixed speed camera in Verwood, Dorset doing 36 mph in a stretch of road where this speed was quite safe. At this time you never know whether a camera is on or off. This is quite stupid. Shortly afterwards I passed a speed camera in Royal Wootton Bassett, and this one was covered up. Dorset Police are out to make money! The fixed penalty had risen from £60 in 2009 to £100 and it is not helping the relationship between drivers and the police.

An advisory speed limit should be given a local trial, similar to those which have been used to test the necessity of white lines which can be reduced in certain places. In other words, they don't always have to be continuous.

One side of a road with no houses/accesses could be 40 mph, while the other side is 30 mph. It wouldn't be difficult to make a change and give it a try. A good example is leaving Coombe Bissett on the A354 Salisbury to Blandford. Drivers are being restricted unnecessarily. Rather than change the signs, '40 MPH' could be painted on that side of the road. If advisory speed limits were to be introduced, this wouldn't be necessary.

The majorities of drivers respect speed limits and would respect advisory limits as well. It is the drivers who do not drive according to the road conditions, which vary continually, who the police should pull over.

I rest my case!

To sum up: advisory speed limits, tougher testing, drive according to road conditions.

For further reading on this important subject please turn to Appendix 6: Further Thoughts on Speeding Motorbikes.

CHAPTER 17

THE WALDEN AND BRUNT FAMILIES
AND OTHER SPECIAL PEOPLE

The paternal grandparents of John Walden

Herbert John Walden (1870–1936), born in Chetnole, Dorset. Moved to Southampton and was involved in the Grocery trade. Later moved to Swindon and then Chute, near Andover. Married Mary Ann Collis from Swansea, South Wales, father of William, Henry John, Gertrude, Florence (Floss), Margery (Marge), Maudeline (Maud), Leslie, Harold and Eveline.

Herbert John Walden, 1936

NB: If you have a subscription to ancestry.co.uk and would like to know more about our origins, to get started search for: Herbert John Walden, born Nov 1871 in Chetnole, Dorset Registration District: Sherborne Father; William Walden, Mother: Elizabeth Curtis. Further information will be found on Walden (Dorset/Wiltshire) Family Tree amongst many other trees researching our family.

Mary Ann, wife of Herbert with Michael.

I am given to understand that the family can be traced back several hundred years and that they were mainly farmers in Dorset. According to the records, there were no bad 'uns' among them! Records show that one branch of the family were producing Butter in Yetminster. Below is a newspaper cutting, kindly sent to me by my cousin Gillian Lock. Gillian, daughter of Leslie Walden, my uncle (see chapter 1), added that my Great Grandfather William "came to a sticky end, poor man, driving his pony and trap home after a few drinks in Yeovil! He was a man of substance and respect – farmer and butcher in the Yetminster area and regularly asked to do Jury duty". (My father Henry also nearly came to a sticky end – he too fell out of a trap but survived, see Chapter 15 "In the saddle".)

NEWSPAPER CUTTING 24/28 July 1891

Fatal Accident – Mr Walden, dairyman of this place, on Friday evening, met with an accident which has terminated fatally. He was returning from Yeovil in his trap, when, on going up Babylon Hill, the trap got too near the bank, with the result that

Mr Walden, who was sitting on a barrel, was thrown out upon the road. The horse continued its journey, eventually reaching home, when Mrs Walden was surprised to see the trap without her husband. She and her son went back to search for Mr Walden, and found him about a mile and a half from the house. He was conveyed home, and Dr Flower attended from Yeovil. It was discovered that a serious injury was sustained to the spine, and the whole of the body from the shoulders was paralyzed. – On Tuesday, an inquest was held before

Mr C.L.O. Bartlett, deputy-coroner of Sherborne, and a jury of whom Mr Gordon Wickham was foreman. Wm. Walden, the deceased's son, was the first witness examined. He said his father's horse arrived home on Friday night about twelve o'clock, but as his father was not in the trap to which the horse was attached, witness went to look for him, and found him lying on his face at the corner of the hill leading to Bradford from Babylon Hill. His father was sensible. With assistance witness got him home, and the next morning went to Yeovil for Dr Flower. – Witness was asked by a juryman the kind of seat his father had in the trap, and he replied that it was a barrel which he had borrowed at Yeovil. His father was a heavy man, and witness conjectured that on the barrel swaying, owing to the trap striking the bank, his father must have lost his balance, and been thrown from the trap. – William Glover, of Yeovil, said deceased was drinking with him at the Globe and Crown on Friday night, and he left there to go home at about five minutes to eleven. He got into the trap and drove off all right. Witness did not consider him the worse for drink, and thought him quite capable of driving himself home. – Dr Flower, of Yeovil, said he was summoned at 10.30 on Saturday morning to Bradford, and he went immediately. He saw the deceased in a sitting-room, where he was lying. His body from the shoulders downwards was paralyzed, owing to the spinal cord being injured. He continued to attend the deceased until death ensued. – The jury returned a verdict of "Accidental death", and added a rider to the effect that they were of the opinion that the turn in the road leading to

Bradford from Babylon Hill was very dangerous to anyone driving there at night, and asking that it should be immediately altered.

The family of Leslie Gordon Walden from left: daughter Gillian, elder son Robert, Robert's wife Stephanie, Timothy and father Leslie. Bluehills, Hilperton, Trowbridge, 1982

The Brunt Family

The pleasant last resting place of Benjamin Brunt 1813-1897 at Glanvilles Wootton, near Sherborne, Dorset. Benjamin farmed at Newlands Farm, Glanvilles Wootton.

Benjamin Brunt. Great Grandfather of the off spring of John Brunt (see below)

The maternal grandparents of John Walden

John Brunt 1847–1933. Born at Haydon Farm, Haydon on Dorset/Somerset border and farmed at Manor Farm, Stalbridge, also in Dorset. Married Agnes. Retired to Park Farm, Frome Road, Trowbridge, Wiltshire.

Lottie died quite young. There was another younger daughter, Mildred, who died at about the age of 17. Apparently she was very pretty. Phyllis, Edna, Hilda and Mildred had lovely auburn hair.

John Brunt and family at Manor Farm, Stalbridge, Dorset, 1914. Back row: Sydney, Lotty, Ralph, Hilton, Marion and Norman, Front row: Hilda, Phyllis and Edna. Centre: John and Agnes.

Manor Farm, Stalbridge, Dorset, where the Brunt family grew up

Top left: Hilda, Grandma Agnes Brunt and Wilfred Giddings, husband of Hilda and father of Gordon, Mary and Neville.

Top right: Granddad John Brunt with Phyllis on right and possibly Norah, daughter of Sydney and his first wife, Mabel.

Lower left: John and Agnes Brunt with Phyllis, age 18 months. Top two photos taken at Park Farm, Trowbridge. Bottom one at Stalbridge.

Henry John Walden (age about 40) 1906-1983, grew up in Chute near Andover Hampshire, Apprenticed to a butter manufacturer (an Uncle) at East Coker, Somerset. Moved to Trowbridge 1925/6. Married Phyllis Harriet Brunt. Father of John, Michael Henry and Benjamin Roger. Henry won a scholarship and attended Andover Grammar School. There being no cars or buses, he rode his pony the nine miles to and fro daily.

Parents of John Walden

Special people

During my 80-odd years there have been quite a number of people who have been a special part of my life. In no particular order, I am sure I have missed some out:

Henry Walden, a good father and mentor; George Olive, an outstanding headmaster; Tony King, my solicitor, neighbour and good friend; My brother Michael; Cousin Donald Walden FCA; Carlo Gondolfi and Harry Fielding, who helped get the poultry business well established; Dennis Gerrish (Waldens Motors Ltd, Garage Manager); Colin White, my first Cold Store Manager; Peter Ainsworth, Waldens' London Sales Manager; Michael Dolman, Building Surveyor; Tony Russell, my brilliant dentist and sailor; Ann, my first wife; John and Elizabeth Meakin, Martin Pound RN; J O Thomas, Principal of Lackham School of Agriculture; Carson and Mildred Patterson,

Canadian farmers; Joe Sutton, American poultry expert. Cousins: Gordon and Neville Giddings, Rosemary and Marion Brunt, Ernie and Jackie Hiscock, John and Gay Tarrant, Bob Huskinson RA and Helen. Sailors: Mike and Jessica Warren, John and Wendy Richardson, Tom and Ros Cunliffe, Mark Woodhouse, Mike and Marion Shaw, Julian Carpenter, Fred and Renee Poynter, Ruth Cotton MBE, Anthea White, Anne Redfern, Lionel and Mary Veck. Doctors:* Rodney Pearce, Paul Hemming, David Ibbitson, Colin Davidson; Mike and Rachel Standish, Phil Bromley, Fred Woodfine, Paul and Marijke Trewick, Francois and Delphine Lance, David and Betty Price, Mike Sanderson, Steve Blake, Martin Darg, Ruth Potter and especially, my children.

*Many NHS doctors have saved my life over the years. I particularly recall Richard Jones at the QA Portsmouth; Edward Barnes, Great Western, Swindon; and Peter Guy, Salisbury. I have reached the ripe age

of 82 only due to the care I received in about nine NHS hospitals, plus two private clinics; doctors, consultants, surgeons and the lovely nurses (including the not so lovely men!) who are in the "front line". Wonderful!

John Tarrant with his sister Margaret on his left and mother Mary on his right. John was a very good farmer and was Chairman of Wiltshire NFU for many years.

Tony King, a great friend and super solicitor (see Chapters 10, 11 and 15). 1988

Charlie Cotton, the son of Ruth, with his wife Katherine. (See Chapter 10)

Fred Poynter and his wife Renee, great friends, 1980. (See Chapters 10 and 12)

Of my close relatives, the following stand out:

Uncles: Norman Brunt, farmer at Tellisford near Bath (soldier at Gallipoli in WW1), father of David, Mark and Norma. His first wife was Rose and his second one was Olive.

Ralph Brunt, Famer at Hilmarton, near Calne and father of Rosemary and Percy (WW2 Mosquito Pilot 'Pathfinder' Killed in action, age 22.)

Sydney Brunt, farmer/market gardener near Faversham in Kent. Had a market stall in Borough Market, London. Father of Marion, Shirley, Juanita, Norman, Neville, Nigel and Norah.

Aunts: Hilda Giddings (mother's sister), of Manor Farm, Sandridge, Melksham. Mother of Mary, Gordon and Neville.

Edna Banwell (mother's sister), mother of Susan. Very kind to me and Michael when we were young.

Four Brunt's: Ralph, Phyllis, Edna and Sydney. On the occasion of Sydney's 80th birthday, 1980

Early days at Downside, the Down. Left: John and Michael in Westholm School caps (see Chapter 5), Phyllis Walden with Michael on her knee and John in his first car. Waldens' factory is in the background. Far right: Michael, Phyllis, Henry and John, 1936-1939

Joseph Henry Walden aged 14. The very special son of John and Barbara Walden

JW with Joseph, age, about two. Photo taken in 1993 at Byebrook Nursing Home, Box, where Phyllis Walden stayed before she passed away at the age of 90. As a baby, Joseph had lovely curly auburn hair, taking after the Brunt family.

JW and daughter Sarah

Below:
From left: Lynsey Boothe age 17, daughter of Rob and Sarah Boothe, with an American friend Chelsea, from Florida. Lynsey is an accomplished Musician. Far right, Sarah with her Husband, Rob.

Banwell and Walden Family picnic at Westwood Farm, Keevil, circa 1936

Sydney and Marion Brunt with JW at Monks Hill Farm, Faversham, 1980

Sydney, Vie and Marion Brunt (age 24) in New Zealand, 1961

Anne Redfern, a good friend, 1980. I was introduced to Anne by my cousin Shirley Brunt. Anne lived at Market Bosworth in Leicestershire. She was great company, but for several reasons we went our separate ways. We remain good friends.°

Below: Hugh and Sarah, children of John and Ann Walden. Growing up!

John Meakin with his sister Ann, my first, and very special wife! After completing his National Service, mostly in Hong Kong, John married Ann's best friend, Elizabeth Heywood. Both were nurses at St Thomas' Hospital in London. Afterwards John and Elizabeth lived in Trinidad for 10 years, where John managed a sugar plantation before returning to Devon and buying a farm. John Walden married Ann in 1956. Right hand photo: A proper soldier!

268

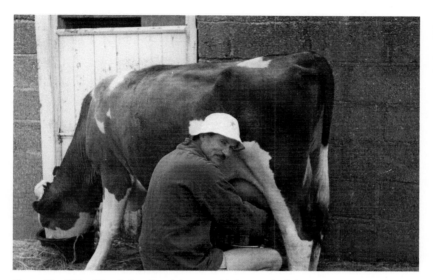

Farmer John (JW) milking Sydney Brunt's house cow (A Simmental called 'Auntie Sim') at Monks Hill Farm, Faversham, Kent.

Top Left: John and Michael, Phyllis at the piano, and Henry. Seated left: Ben with Chaser, a Norwich terrier

A couple of love birds! JW couldn't resist including this amorous photo of Henry and Phyllis taken at the rear of Downside, The Down, Trowbridge. Circa 1945.

Norah Trigg

John Trigg, Husband of Norah. During the Blitz of Bath, in followed by Bristol and then Cardiff, during WW2 John was based at RAF Colerne, near Bath. He gave the Luftwaffe a run for their money. Before he landed at Colerne he often flew at zero feet over Downside, the home of the Walden family, where Norah stayed during the war, to let her know that he would soon be home.

Percy Brunt age 22 in 1942, son of Ralph and Winnie Brunt and brother of Rosemary. In WW2 Percy was a Pathfinder pilot flying Mosquitos. He was very special. I stayed at Catcombe Farm, Hilmarton, when I was about four years old and Percy would have been 16.

Percy was the only son of Ralph and Winnie Brunt. In 1939 at the age of 19 he joined the RAF Volunteer Reserve. At one stage he was sent to the USA to train American pilots, particularly in air warfare gunnery, before becoming a Pathfinder flying a Mosquito. Pathfinders generally flew ahead of the main bomber formations and lit the targets with flares dropped by parachute. The Mosquitos were unarmed. I gathered from his father, my Uncle Ralph, that in 1944 aged 24 Percy had completed two x 30 missions over Germany. On returning from the last sortie, dense fog covered the runway at his base which was RAF Gravely, near Huntingdon. Ahead of Percy another aircraft had crashed on the runway. The Control Tower radioed to Percy to abort his landing and gain height pronto. It was too late. There was a tree at the end of the runway and Percy crashed into it. He was killed outright. Flying Officer Percy Brunt is buried in the Cambridge City Cemetery. His main claim to fame is probably that his letters to his fiancée are preserved in the Imperial War Museum in London. (His fiancée was Ragland Newman-Nugas, an attractive Scandinavian lass in the WRENS, attached to the Admiralty)

A Mosquito as flown by Percy Brunt and John Trigg. Mosquitos were built of wood and constructed in two halves before being joined together!

John Brunt, the elder son of Hylton Brunt, who served throughout WW2 in the RAF Regiment. Top left photo: On guard. Top photo: Flying Officer: Left photo: Farmer John.

272

The following was kindly provided by John's daughter, Anne-Marie Nash:

"My parents were planning to marry in early 1940 in Borehamwood, Herts, where my mother lived. At that time my father worked for his father running the milk delivery business associated with his farm. On the outbreak of war the wedding was brought forward and took place on September 7th 1939, 3 days after war was declared. My father joined up in January 1940. He wanted to be a pilot but mercifully his eyesight was not good enough. He joined the RAF Regiment as a private instead. In the early years of the war he was involved in extensive training in numerous locations around southern and eastern England and undertook a lengthy stint on convoy protection duty making countless trips by ship between Sheerness and Southampton in all weathers.

He obtained several promotions and by the time he crossed to Normandy several days after D Day he had the rank of Flying Officer. He took an RAF Regiment unit across the Channel with the role of defending airfields newly built behind the advancing Allied front line. He was sometimes billeted with farming families as they moved across country and into Belgium, and he found their farms and orchards very interesting because of his background. Eventually they reached Brussels, where they stayed for a while and the local inhabitants gave them a terrific welcome. The family of a Belgian Baron, were especially hospitable. I think that by then the war was almost over. However it was some months later before he was demobbed. By that time he had moved on further, spending quite some time in Germany on the Lüneburg Heath and eventually left for England from the Isle of Sylt in Schleswig Holstein."

John Brunt's wedding on the 7th September, 1939, before he joined the RAF.
John's dad, Hylton Brunt, elder of the Brunt brothers and uncle of JW, is on the far left.

Norman and Rose Brunt with their son David. Circa 1937

WW1, The Dorset Regiment prior to service in Gallipoli. Norman Brunt is in the middle row next to the motorbike.

David Brunt, son of Norman, was called up in 1943.

David Brunt (middle, front row) at the RCAF Base at Brandon, Ontario, Canada, where he trained to be a pilot. Once he had his "Wings" he flew a Canadian-built Liberator Bomber to the UK. Luckily for David the war had come to an end.

Mark Brunt's marriage to Gillian. From left: Norman Brunt, Connie, (Gill's mum) Mark and Gillian, Olive, (Norman's second wife) and Dick, Gillian's Dad. 4th January 1969

Phyllis Harriet Walden, mother of John, Michael and Ben, on her 80th birthday. Photo taken at Halfway Cottage, Hilperton Road Trowbridge.

JW with his mother, Phyllis, 1960

David and Ruby Brunt, on the occasion of their marriage at Tellisford, near Bath.

John Walden with Pickles, 1980. Pickles came from the home of Sydney and Betty Dawson, the parents of Anne Redfern, who was a good friend in my second bachelor days! Eventually, I gave Pickles to my son Hugh when he moved to Lowestoft to study at the International Boat Building School. Hugh stayed in a camper van which he had converted from a van, complete with a wood-burning stove. This super dog was great company for Hugh.
Unfortunately Pickles tried to swallow a sharp bone and sadly choked to death.

Neville Giddings, (son of Wilfred and Hilda (nee Brunt) with from left: daughter Stephanie, wife Ruth and daughter Angela. Photo taken by JW at Chalcot Park Farm, near Westbury, Wiltshire. Summer 2014

The following photos are of Ralph Brunt and his family. Kindly sent to me by his daughter Rosemary.

Top left: Percy on leave from the RAF
Top right: farmer Ralph Brunt, at Chase Farm Fernhurst;
Above: Ralph, Rosemary and Percy
Left: Rosemary holding Grumpy, Percy's springer spaniel.

Rosemary at Chase Farm, Fernhurst, age 33

Ralph with prize cauliflowers he had grown
at Catcombe Farm, Spirthill, Hilmarton,
Calne. Rosemary and Percy at Catcombe.
Both attended the John Bentley School in
Calne, which, at that time, was on the Green.

Percy, aged 16,
with Ben and
Judy at Catcombe.

1917 'tractor' at
Stalbridge, Ralph
driving. (Ralph built
this tractor from a
Model T Ford.)

Percy at rear of cart, Rosemary in front at Loverly Farm.

Percy driving tractor age 6 at Loverly Farm, Crichel, near Wimborne, Dorset (the little girl on the left is Rosemary at two years old). Bottom: 1927 at Loverly Farm, Crichel.

Rosemary and Ralph Brunt at Slinden after Ralph had retired

Neville Brunt, son of Sydney and his first wife Mabel, (centre standing); from left is Norah Brunt, Phyllis Walden, unknown, Vera Brunt, Neville's wife. Neville was in a Tank Regiment throughout the North African Campaign where he was awarded the "Oakleaf" for outstanding bravery. Towards the end of the war he transferred to the Parachute Regiment.

John Walden, age 82, with youngest son Joseph, age 24, 2014

Sydney "Norman" Brunt, elder son of Sydney, with his wife Joyce. Norman was a prominent breeder of Large White pigs, which he showed at major agricultural shows. Later he became a senior judge of pigs and Dexter cattle.

Joseph (Joe) Walden on his trials racing bike. A very dangerous sport which I am pleased to say he had given up. He has also given up riding motorbikes on the highway, thank goodness!

JW's son Sam, age 28, with girlfriend Hannah, taken at the Ship, Upavon, on JW's 82nd birthday, 2014

Sam, Dad John and Joseph Walden at Upavon 2013

Susan (daughter of Donald and Edna Banwell) and Asa (Lord and Lady Briggs)age 81 and 92, circa 2012.

JW's eldest son Hugh with his wife Rebecca and dogs, Doris on left and Rummage, taken at Damerham in May 2014

Happy days at Westwood Farm, Keevil. Left: farmer Susan. Middle: JW, Michael, mother Phyllis, Susan with her mother Edna Banwell in the Hayfield. Right: Michael, Susan and John perched on a hen coop, 1937

Neville Giddings with his brother Gordon (see Chapter 15)

Westwood Farm, Keevil, near Trowbridge. Home of the Banwell family

"A-hunting we will go" - Gordon and Neville on their horses, 1955

Back row: Paul Stumbles, Wilfred Giddings, Gordon and Gill Giddings. Front row: Mary Stumbles (nee Giddings), Hilda Giddings, Mary Webb and, hard right, her husband Bernard. Circa 1950

Clockwise from left: Dr Barbara Walden, Gillian Walden, Michael and John, 1986.

Back row: Bob Wyatt, Paul Stumbles, Henry John Walden. Middle row: Antony and Neil Stumbles. Sitting on step: Marion Wyatt (née Brunt), Girlie, Phyllis Walden with Sarah (JW's daughter) on her knee, Mary Stumbles and Granny, Winifred / Wilfie Heard, née Stumbles. Taken at the Bournemouth home of Bob and Marion Wyatt, probably by Jacqueline Stumbles (now Barton). Circa 1966.

Michael Henry Walden, age 81, and his wife Gillian, 2014

At the Pepper Mill, (Not the Pepper Pot!) Devizes, August 2014. From left, Michael Walden, his wife Gillian, JW, Gay Tarrant and her plumptious husband, John

The last photo of Michael Henry Walden, 1933-2014. Taken at The Elms, Keevil, where he had lived for 50 years.

Two octogenarians, JW and Michael

For further interest:

Michael, at the age of 16, signed up as an apprentice in the Merchant Navy and joined the Tanker *Athol Regent* in Liverpool. This vessel was bound for the Persian Gulf, where it loaded crude oil. The destination was the River Plate in Argentina/Uruguay. The *Athol Regent* made several voyages between the Persian Gulf and South America before returning to Liverpool after a year at sea. Michael decided that the Merchant Navy wasn't for him. He returned to Trowbridge and made himself useful in the family business before being called up for National Service at the age of 18. He joined the 11th Hussars, an Armoured Regiment, beginning his training at Catterick in Yorkshire before being sent to Germany. Later he was stationed at Warminster. During training on Salisbury Plain he was reported for shooting rabbits. He was disciplined by a senior officer who admonished him, "Walden, you don't appear to be taking your Army duties seriously. You are confined to Barracks for 7 days and will do 4 hours' drill each day" (square bashing!). Michael was adventurous, and disliked being tied down, either in his business life or private one. He was somewhat non-conformist and often politically incorrect. He was, however, very genuine, kind and a good family man. He raised two fine daughters, Sally, a financial wizard, and

Tessa who became a C of E Vicar. He was respected and well-liked by his colleagues and staff. When he was fully involved in running one of the Walden Group of Companies, firstly Waldens Eggs Ltd., and latterly the four Supermarkets, he was always professional and successful. In his younger days, when driving his car through Marlborough, he was "pulled over" for exceeding the 30 MPH limit. He had to appear before the Magistrates and during the brief hearing he told the Court "The law is an Ass". (JW would agree with him particularly in relation to Speed Limits!) which, understandably, made Headlines in the National Press. Much later he was elected as a Councilor during which time he set sail in his yacht "*Trimley Maid*" to the Caribbean for ten months. Again, this made Headlines. Michael was very intelligent, great company, and for me, a smashing Brother.

Tom and Ros Cunliffe. Tom is a famous yachtsman, author and orator. Ros is a lovely lady! (See Chapter 13)

Michael Walden, age 18 in his Army uniform.

Commander Martin Pound R.N. Martin was a senior Navigator in the Royal Navy and saw service on the Royal Yacht Britannia. (See Chapter 13) Top left photo taken on HMS Endurance, 1987, bottom left one as Navigating Officer on HMAS Jarvis Bay and right one as Captain of a Minesweeper HMS Walkerton 1976. Martin's ancestors were Royal Navy Officers going back several generations, His father was a captain and his grandfather was Admiral of the Fleet Sir Dudley Pound, who was prominent in the early part of WW2.

Four Brunt sisters: Marion, Edna, Phyllis and Hilda, 1923

left: Marion Brunt (One of the Brunt sisters) at Church Farm, Tellisford, near Bath. JW and his brother Michael used to camp there and swim in the River Frome which bordered the farm. The centre photo is Norman Brunt, who served in the Wiltshire Yeomanry in WW1 at Gallipoli and later farmed at Church Farm. His son David was a Liberator Bomber pilot in WW2. The right photo of the three is Sydney Brunt.

Where the Brunt sisters went to school. Sherborne Convent, about 1910

Three Brunt sisters, Hilda, Edna and Phyllis, at Marion's wedding

Wilfred Giddings, Donald Banwell, Edna Banwell, 1925. In front: Hilda Giddings. Donald and Edna Banwell farmed at Westwood Farm, Keevil near Trowbridge. JW often stayed there and taught their daughter Susan long division! Susan later married the historian Lord Asa Briggs. Edna made Cheddar cheese and super ice-cream.

Winnie and Percy Brunt, 1944, and Winnie with Percy as a Baby in 1922

John Meakin, age 81, and
John Walden, age 82

From left: Robert Meakin, JW, Heather Meakin, Elizabeth Meakin
and John Meakin. Photo taken at the Funeral of John Meakin's
brother Dick at Minety, 24th June 2014

Where there's muck there's money! John Meakin
with some of his dairy cows at Middle Radom
Farm, Lewdown, near Okehampton in Devon,
1984. In 1988 John sold his cows and changed to
sheep and rearing and fattening beef calves, which
did very well on his very rich grassland.

John and Elizabeth Meakin at Tavistock 2014

Mary, Rosie, Elsie Ann,
Granddad Hugh Walden
and Nancy. Photo taken
at Elsie Ann's christening,
July 6th 2014

The Brunt and Walden family reunion at the Compasses Inn, Damerham, June 15th 2014. Back row from left: Anthony Brunt, son of Neville and Vera Brunt; Rebecca and Hugh Walden, son of JW; Norman Boxall, partner of Jill Fenwick; Amanda, wife of Anthony Brunt; John Penniceard, Husband of Judith; Marianne, daughter of Nigel Brunt and granddaughter of Sydney, with her husband, Michael Schoenig. Middle row from left: Harriet, daughter of Laura Trigg and granddaughter of Sydney Brunt; Rosie, daughter of Hugh and Rebecca Walden; Gillian, daughter of Rosemary and granddaughter of Ralph Brunt; Marion Brunt, daughter of Sydney; Rosemary, daughter of Ralph Brunt; Jill Fenwick, daughter of Norman Brunt, Granddaughter of Sydney; Laura Trigg, daughter of Norah Trigg and granddaughter of Sydney; Judith Penniceard, daughter of Norman, granddaughter of Sydney; Ruth Giddings, wife of Neville. Front row seated: Vera, widow of Neville Brunt; Neville Giddings, son of Hilda Brunt. Between them is Isabel, daughter of Marianne and Michael Schoenig. JW took the photo.

JW with his good friend Anthea White and her dog Bertie. Summer 2013

JW's 80th birthday celebration at the Bear Hotel, Devizes, January 2012. JW, John Tarrant, Michael Walden. Front row: Anthea White, Gay Tarrant, Gillian Walden.

Jackie and Ernie Hiscock at the Ship, Upavon, 2012

Phillip Bromley, a great friend when one was needed most! 2009

Betty Price, a very good friend. Betty owns and runs a very special ladies' boutique called Jessica's in Fordingbridge, which attracts customers over a 50-mile radius. She is a stalwart in the social life of the town. Betty's Husband David is a retired Master Butcher. Circa 2014

Gil Rooke, his wife Lynn, JW and his eldest son Hugh, 2012 (Heddington)

Mike Sanderson. A good friend and top class IT expert! Mike was a great help in the preparation of this book.

Martin Darg, Managing Director of Astute Enterprises Ltd. Martin is a professional web designer who has prepared and updates my website at www.gogreenadventurecamping.co.uk

APPENDIX 1

Waldens' final years

Following JW's retirement, which was partially due to ill health, Ben took over the reins with a vengeance. In the years when I was involved everything developed steadily and successfully. It was very well established at this time, and Ben certainly continued the progress. My cousin Donald retired at the same time. A new accountant was appointed, Bob Livingstone, who had previously been with Unilever. Bearing in mind his background his approach to the family business was quite different to that of mine and Donald's. I am sure he influenced Ben in the direction he was to follow.

The first thing they did was to wind up Frigfreight, replace the fleet of vehicles with hired ones and close down the garage. As the eventual buyer would not have required Frigfreight and would set up their own distribution operation, Frigfreight could have been sold off as a going concern. It definitely had great potential. I felt that this was a waste of my efforts, which disgusted me. The previous set-up had worked very well for 35 years and was definitely one of the major activities which ensured the success of the Walden Group.

Michael was left without a joB&Ben was pleased that I was no longer involved. Ben's objective was to prepare the business for sale, which he did. When I retired he paid himself at least twice the salary I had received. Right throughout my 35 years with the firm the three brothers had equal shares in the company. With the extra money in his pocket, Ben set about buying all the 'loose' shares from several Aunts. Mother gave him her Shares and Father gave him a 3-acre paddock. Quite a degree of favouritism!

In the space of a few years Ben took steps to find a buyer for the business. Brake brothers made an offer, which wasn't accepted. Very soon Carl Dusterburg of apetito (Germany) came on the scene. He had visited us some years earlier. This time he came with his cheque book and paid 14 million pounds sterling for the business. A large chunk of this had to be repaid to ICFC, who had a substantial holding in the firm in return for lending a large sum.

On completion of the sale, Ben expected to be the Chief Executive of apetito UK. Unfortunately this didn't work out as he had planned and his term with apetito was quite short. I am told he was very upset! Personally, I am not unduly surprised that he was relieved of his post as it is very rare that a managing director of a business is retained following a takeover. I had a similar experience when I was sacked by Ross Group when they took over the Waldens Poultry business. The only difference was that I was quite pleased!

When I retired the business was employing about 650 people, and this was still the case when it was sold. Apetito bought an exceptionally good company which had developed from a tiny acorn sown in 1926. They are now employing over 1200 people (see their website www.apetito.com and/or www.en.wikipedia.org.wiki/apetito). Worldwide they currently employ nearly 9,000 and I am pleased to report that they are good employers.

At the time of the sale I was not particularly well. Ben came to see me to tell me he had a buyer, which I thought was fine. He didn't tell me that he now owned far more shares than either Michael or me. It was an underhand move. The outcome was that Ben pocketed £6m from the sale, whereas Michael and I received £1m each. Not quite equitable! He had stolen the family silver. This is something which neither Michael nor I would have done.

Water under the bridge – family businesses do have their problems, but Ben's action has left a rather bitter taste in both Michael's and my mouths. That's life, I guess. One fact which slightly offsets this injustice is that Ben organized a sensible pension for us both. It is certainly appreciated, but it has not squared the books.

Throughout my long, generally happy and active life, my motto has always been 'Do unto others as you will be done by'. It is a great pity that Ben didn't practise the same!

APPENDIX 2

Introducing **Go Green Adventure Camping (GGAC)**

(NB: This is primarily for farmers and landowners (FLO's), as well as adventurous campers!)

While I was involved in the development and running of Blackland Lakes (See Chapter 12) at Calne, I considered ways of offering adventurous people who preferred to be independent, the means of camping on farms as an alternative to commercial campsites. On my retirement from Blackland Lakes, I set about getting the idea established. This was in 2011. Now, in 2014, it is well established. There is still, however, considerably more scope, particularly for additional camping venues, both in the UK, Eire and further afield.

My experience so far is very encouraging. The scheme is attracting the type of individuals who appreciate the opportunity to camp independently of the 'madding crowd', rather like me! The feedback from both campers and landowners is very positive. It is attracting decent families and friends.

From the FLO point of view it is not a 'big earner', although the bookings, which are prepaid via PayPal, are a useful source of extra income. The main point is that it is giving adventurous, independent individuals the opportunity to enjoy the countryside and at the same time to learn more about how food is produced. FLOs often meet some quite interesting folk!

View www.gogreenadventurecamping.co.uk, find the FLO section, scroll down to how to join the GGAC Association and click to bring up a questionnaire. Complete this and email it to JW Leisure Ltd. It is easy and, currently, free, to join the Go Green Adventure Association and welcome independent and adventurous campers.

The more choice GGAC can offer the better for everyone. No planning permission is required. The 1932 Public Health Act still applies. JW Leisure will welcome enquiries from Farmers and Landowners and bookings from adventurous Campers

APPENDIX 3

Some reflections on a long and interesting life*(NB: This is primarily for*

I have noticed that there are quite a number of decent young individuals who have taken up an academic training, often at a university, at great expense, either to themselves or the taxpayer, when they are obviously not cut out for this type of career. It would be far better for them to take practical training and make a good fist of that, where there is plenty of scope and a shortage of labour. With due diligence they can still rise to the top!

The trouble often is that after all this studying they are frequently not equipped for a career which would be more suitable for them. They often get disenchanted and sometimes take a detrimental turn in their lives. Before they start their adult education they should be given advice to try and guide them towards a career which is suited to their talent, their choice of the route to follow and the likelihood of them being successful. Perhaps an opportunity should be given to allow them to experience life in the field of their choice to give them a chance of demonstrating that they fit the establishment and the establishment fits them. This could avoid a lot of wasted time and money. It is always preferable if they can follow something they are interested in, something which is more likely to give them job satisfaction and a happy working life.

During my business career I have met several over-educated individuals who just didn't fit in and they were generally not much help to an employer or to themselves. This could have been avoided if they had been guided into something better suited to their talent and ability. A lot of work needs to be done in this area. I am sure it is much better today than it was 40 or 50 years ago. It needs to be very carefully monitored.

Over the years, there are one or two proverbs or sayings which I have always kept in mind. The first is 'Do unto others as you would be done by' and the other is 'Money is the root of all evil'. In my case both are important and, at times, both have had an effect on my life, good and bad!

Young people should travel as much as possible before they become tied down with family and work commitments and responsibilities. Accept any work at the bottom of the ladder until an opportunity presents itself which attracts you. It doesn't always happen overnight. Likewise businesses often take a considerable time to become successful and profitable. Profit is not a dirty word. To make progress and to stay in business it is vital.

Another point which I have recognized is that there are many people over the age of 65 who are quite capable of holding down responsible jobs. They should not be written off without giving the matter very careful consideration. Some deteriorate very quickly, but there are many others who can be very valuable to employers and often can help younger colleagues. It must be taken into account that they have had many years of experience and knowledge which takes years and years to acquire. You are never too old to learn.

Never give up and keep smiling!

APPENDIX 4

A proposal aimed at reducing accidents and unnecessary deaths of motorcyclists, death or serious injury to other road users and the resulting cost and grief which this causes

The proposal put forward below has been prompted by the untimely death of my son Sam, who crashed on the way to a race meeting in Belgium on the 6th August 2014. Unfortunately, with Sam, as with quite a large number of owners of powerful motorbikes, the excitement of high speed became an obsession. As his younger brother Joseph pointed out, 'Sam couldn't get enough of it'.

I have noticed for a long time that too many riders of powerful motorbikes ride them at high speed, even when there is a considerable amount of other traffic. When you are passed by two or more of these bikes (even one is bad enough) the noise they generate is horrendous. As it appears to come from nowhere and is very sudden, the shock to drivers which they are passing is quite frightening.

The writer's view of the above is that it is a form of anti-social behaviour, even a criminal offence, which should not be tolerated. I am not against motorcyclists, the majority of whom ride at sensible speeds and do not cause problems. It is the speed merchants who need to receive attention.

Over the past five years I have been caught speeding in my car at 38 and 36 mph in two 30 mph zones. Both were in areas where these speeds were quite safe when judged by the prevailing road conditions. I was definitely not causing any danger to other road users. For the first infringement I was given the option of a £100 fine plus three points or a fine of £70 and a day's training course. I chose the latter, which proved to be quite sensible. For the more recent infringement I paid the excessive £100 fine and gritted my teeth!

Had advisory speed limits been in force, I would not have been fined. Any dangerous driving would, of course, be treated as a serious offence and this would be reflected in the punishment. This would save, not only valuable police time, but remove a massive amount of bureaucratic rubbish, plus the unnecessary stress which it causes on the affected motorist.

Possible short and long-term solution

1. All owners of motorbikes of 350cc and over should be made to take a course run by the Institute of Advance Motoring before they are allowed to ride on the public highway.

2. All riders apprehended for causing anti-social behaviour (or dangerous driving) as outlined above, should be given the option of accepting a fine of, say, £150 or alternatively take the course run by the IAM, for which they would pay. If this course is introduced, similar to the present one, for minor infringements of the present outdated limits, I am sure there will be a quite rapid improvement in the standard of riding motorbikes. In addition, and very much more important, the loss of life will be significantly reduced which is the main objective,

I would like the new law to be known as 'Sam's Law' in memory of my son, Sam.

APPENDIX 5

To reduce carbon emissions – a proposal for consideration:

Introducing the "Village Combination"

Over the past several years village shops, post offices, pubs and petrol stations have been closing, one after the other. This is causing considerable unnecessary travelling which can and should be avoided.

The following would be a solution. In the principal village of a given area, say a 5 mile radius, a combination unit should be established. This would comprise: a small well stocked shop/post office, a pub/eating place, a doctor's surgery, a filling station and a community "taxi". All would be under one general manager/owner (not run by a committee, a limited company is preferable). It should make a viable, profitable business.

The filling station would be "self-service" and unmanned. Deliveries could be via local heating fuel suppliers. Customers would pay by their bank card. This would reduce carbon emissions substantially and be a great service for the locals, particularly the elderly. Whilst the interior of the unit would be right up to date, the exterior should be designed to blend in with the rest of the village and not stick out like a sore thumb. A "horse port" should be provided so that those choosing to travel on horseback, either for pleasure or to do business, could do so, and enjoy a pint or two and a sausage roll in the pub. The surgery could be linked to a central one in the locality and would possibly only open two days per week. All the rest would open daily. If a pub, closed or open, still exists, this would be the ideal focal point of any development.

The above would reduce traffic both on country roads and in the towns and cities. Who is going to lead the field?

APPENDIX 6

JW's views on the European Union, the "Uncommon Market"!

I have noticed ever since Ted Heath took us into the "Common Market" that:

1. It is not a common market as was the intention. It is just a bureaucratic nightmare.

2. The UK has been an uncomfortable member from the outset.

3. It is causing a division within the UK population which is neither helpful nor needed.

4. If we stay in it this will continue and get worse.

5. We should get out and form a separate "common market" with elected members only.

6. It could be a free trade organization which all EU members will be free to join. It could encompass any country who wished to join, especially the USA and members of the Commonwealth. Even China and Russia?

7. The main benefit of the UK being a member of the EU is that it has helped keep the peace. We could be an associate member if it survives, involved in stability/peace oriented projects and definitely NATO.

8. If we stay in, the UK will never be at ease.

9. The Conservative Party, with main party support, should take the initiative and not leave it to UKIP, who, in my view, are largely made up of misfits and opportunists. They are not in a position to govern the UK.

10. For thousands of years Britain has ruled itself, mainly successfully. The British people do not want, or need, to be ruled by others. We beat the Nazis. Now we should extract ourselves from the latest "enemy"- not the people, the bureaucrats.